Letters from an Old Orangeman

CLASSICS OF IRISH HISTORY
General Editor: Ciaran O'Brady

Original publication dates of reprinted titles are given in brackets

Michael Davitt, *Jottings in Solitary*
George Moore, *Parnell and His Island* (1887)
Charlotte Elizabeth Tonna, *Irish Recollections* (1841/47 as *Personal Recollections*)
Standish James O'Grady, *Sun and Wind*
John Sarsfield Casey, *The Galtee Boy: A Fenian Prison Narrative*
William and Mary Ann Hanbidge, *Memories of West Wicklow: 1813–1939* (1939)
A. P. A. O'Gara, *The Green Republic* (1902)
William Cooke Taylor, *Reminiscences of Daniel O'Connell* (1847)
William Bruce and Henry Joy, *Belfast Politics* (1794)
Annie O'Donnell, *Your Fondest Annie*
Joseph Keating, *My Struggle for Life* (1916)
John Mitchel, *The Last Conquest of Ireland (Perhaps)* (1858/9)
Harold Begbie, *The Lady Next Door* (1914)
Eugene Davis, *Souvenirs of Footprints Over Europe* (1889)
Maria Edgeworth, *An Essay on Irish Bulls* (1802)
D. P. Moran, *The Philosophy of Irish Ireland* (1898–1900)
T. M. Kettle, *The Open Secret of Ireland* (1912)
David W. Miller, *Queen's Rebels* (1978)
Frank Frankfort Moore, *In Belfast by the Sea*
Ernie O'Malley, *Rising Out: Seán Connolly of Longford*
John Devoy, *Michael Davitt: 'From the Gaelic American'*
Richard Twiss, *A Tour in Ireland in 1775* (1776)
Wilfrid Ewat, *A Journey in Ireland 1921* (1922)
Sir John Pope Hennessy, *Sir Walter Ralegh in Ireland* (1922)
Patrick Pearse, *Short Stories* (1917)
James Stephens, *The Birth of the Fenian Movement*
Charles Stewart Parnell, *Words of the Dead Chief*, compiled by Jennie Wyse-Power (1892)
John Joseph Horgan, *Parnell to Pearse* (1949)
Darrel Figgis, *A Chronicle of Jails* (1917)
John Sarsfield Casey, *A Mingling of Swans: A Cork Fenian and Friends 'visit' Australia*
J. F. X. O'Brien, *For the Liberty of Ireland at Home and Abroad*
James Fintan Lalor, *'The Faith of a Felon' and Other Writings*
Frances Taylor, *Irish Homes and Irish Hearts* (1867)
Patrick S. Dinneen, *The Queen of the Hearth* (1915)

Letters from an Old Orangeman (1836)

Montanus

With an introduction and notes by Marc Mulholland

UNIVERSITY COLLEGE DUBLIN PRESS
PREAS CHOLÁISTE OLLSCOILE BHAILE ÁTHA CLIATH
2025

First published in 1836
This edition first published by
University College Dublin Press, 2025

ISBN 978-1-0685023-2-3
ISSN 1393–6883

University College Dublin Press
UCD Humanities Institute, Room H103
Belfield,
Dublin 4
www.ucdpress.ie

CIP data available from the British Library

Typeset in Ehrhardt in Dublin by Shane Gough
Text design by Lyn Davies
Printed in Ireland on acid-free paper by
Sprintprint, Cookstown Industrial Estate,
Tallaght, Dublin 24, Ireland

Image Opposite Introductory Essay
'Loyal Orange Lodge Certificate for Stephen Simmons, 1814', courtesy of St Neots Cambridgeshire Community Archive Network

Contents

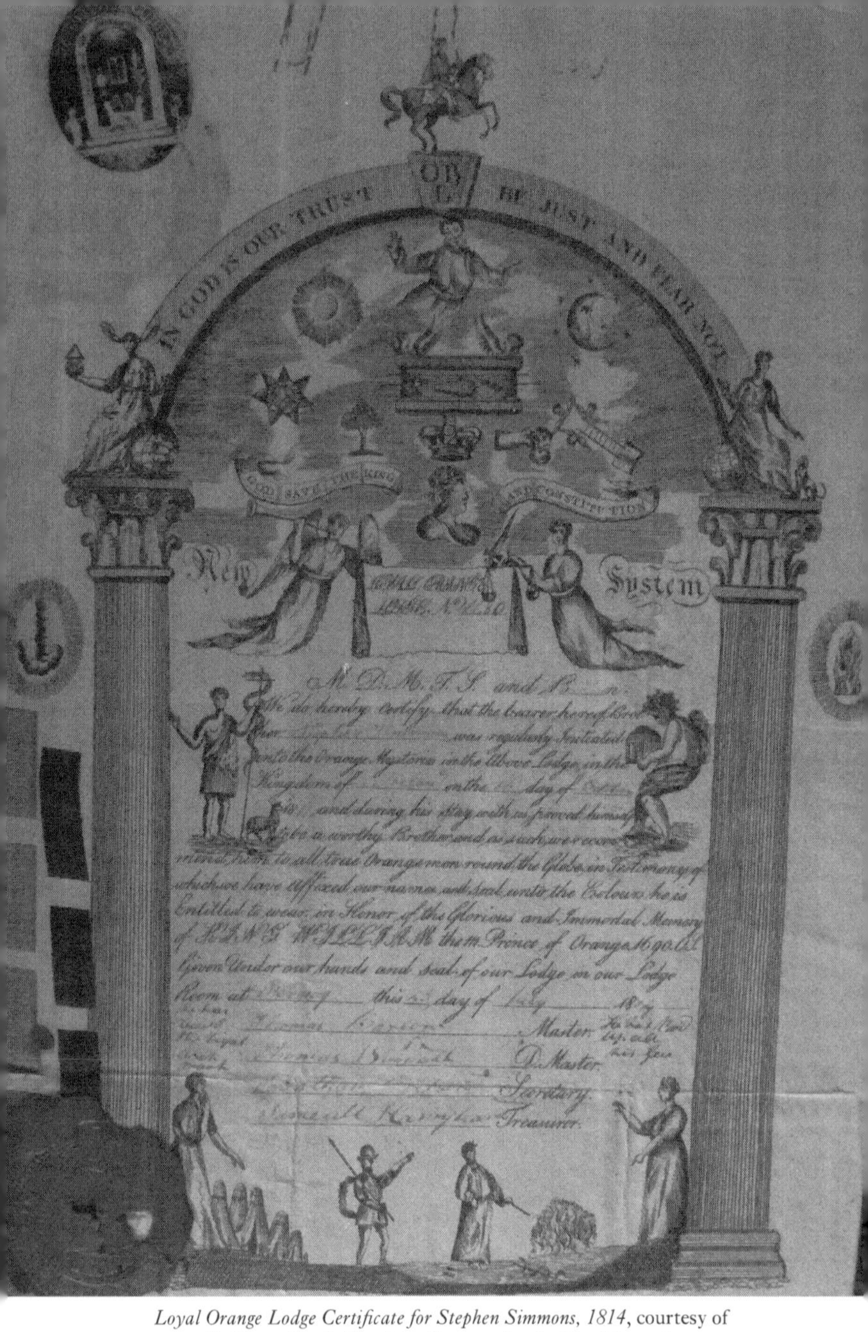

Loyal Orange Lodge Certificate for Stephen Simmons, 1814, courtesy of St Neots Cambridgeshire Community Archive Network

Introductory Essay

Marc Mulholland

THE LETTERS

In April 1835, the *Dublin University Magazine*, an intellectual journal that combined unbending Protestantism with Irish cultural patriotism, published a lengthy article claiming to answer the question 'What is an Orangeman?'[1] This piece was in many ways characteristic of the journal: a defence of the Protestant ascendancy and ultra-Tory principles combined with a genuine fascination with the culture and dynamics of Irish peasant society. It was not merely a reflective journalism, however. It was intended as an urgent intervention: defence and defiance in the face of an existential threat to the 40-year-old Orange Order.

Since the rise of Daniel O'Connell's Catholic Association in the 1820s, 'Orange oppression' had been a staple of nationalist propaganda in Ireland. It was repeatedly asserted, with considerable truth, that the Orange Order acted as a semi-secret society permeating and twisting the judiciary and administration of Ireland. Juries 'packed' with Orangemen, Orange magistrates, Orange lodges in the army, covert Orange influence on ministers and civil servants at Dublin Castle, and an official paramilitary 'Yeomanry' which was indistinguishable from Orangemen in government uniform, were all cited as dangerous and corrupting subversions of law and liberty. Nationalist anger might be taken for granted by their enemies, even welcomed. More dangerous, from the point of view of the Orange Order, was the rising tide of concern in Great Britain. Here Radical MPs had long suspected the Order of seeking to frustrate any and all progressive reform. Orangemen, it was well-known, were organising the rougher Protestant migrants from Ireland in London, Liverpool and Glasgow. The Order had infiltrated the Army and was recruiting men and officers. Orange support reached up into the aristocracy and even the Royal Family. Rumours swirled that Orange conspirators had attempted to organise a royal coup d'état to prevent passage of the mildly democratising 'Great Reform Act' of 1832. Having won a landslide victory in the subsequent general election, the Whigs saw an opportunity to stamp out the Orange threat once and for all. In 1835, a Select Committee of the House of Commons was established to conduct an investigation into Orange activities in both islands. Everybody expected the process to end with the Order being made illegal.

The *DUM*'s article, therefore, was intended as a last-ditch defence of the institution. It came in direct response to the deluge of unedifying evidence being dragged into the light of day by the proceedings of the Select Committee. As a counter-strike it was formidable and, in its own way, impressive. Kevin Haddick-Flynn has described the article, itself deeply indebted to a paper delivered by Rev. Mortimer O'Sullivan, chaplain to the Orange Order, as 'the fullest apologia for Orangeism written in the 19th century'.[2] Of even greater interest to the historian, however, was the series of 'Three Letters from an Old Orangeman' that followed in the August, September and October issues of the *DUM*. These articles have never been republished and have been almost entirely overlooked in writings about the Orange Order. They are, however, a key source.

'Old Orangeman', signed himself as 'Montanus' of County Down, a reference to a prophet of the second century of the Christian Era who Protestants numbered as a forerunner of their own purified faith. Old Orangeman revealed that he was aged 87 at the time of writing, which would have given him a birth-date of around 1748. He had been a mature man of 30 when the Protestant and patriotic Irish Volunteer movement appeared in 1778, and 34 when the combination of Henry Grattan's oratorical skill and the Volunteers' military menace won legislative independence for the Irish Parliament in 1782. Up to middle-age he had supported the 'phantom delusions' of Grattan's movement, but as Ireland spiralled towards separatist revolution in the 1790s, Montanus recoiled. When the Orange Order was established in 1795, Old Orangeman was already aged about 47. 'I knew its founders, most of whom were my personal friends; and I have watched its workings.'[3]

Apologies for the Order, both contemporary and modern, have tended to rely heavily on two argumentative strategies.[4] First, Orangeism is typically characterised as a harmless or at least moderating tradition within loyalism. Second, in an incessant recourse to *tu quoque*, the sectarianism and aggression of Catholic and nationalist rivals are cited as balancing or over-balancing any Orange excess. These argumentative strategies were the gravamen of the *DUM*'s first article, 'What is an Orangeman?', and have been the load-bearing element of apologias ever sense. They are rooted in an age of romantic historicism, taking shape as the Order first flourished and skilfully represented in the pages of the *DUM*, which vindicated each living tradition as necessarily valid in its own terms and ranked them, by a kind of double-entry accounting, by their contributions to civility and civilisation. This approach can certainly be found in Old Orangeman's Letters, which seek to contrast the stabilising and defensive essence of the Orange

Order against the medieval theology of Roman Catholicism and the barbaric savagery of the Catholic peasantry.

Montanus, however, had grown to maturity in the years of Enlightenment rationalism, and this adds an intriguing dimension to his work. He subscribed to the eighteenth-century idea, which always remained strong in Ireland, that human nature is universal but variously cramped or liberated by the moulding context of interest and ideology. Montanus, it is clear, was steeped in Enlightenment optimism, even if it had long curdled in him. He was fully alive to the attractiveness not only of the militant Patriotism in the mould of Henry Grattan, which was by no means superficial, but even of the republican separatism evinced by the United Irishmen. His perceptive characterisation of Theobald Wolfe Tone is perhaps not what one would expect of a fervent loyalist:

> Wolfe Tone was a man of spirit and humanity. He possessed the enthusiasm of a poet, and the enterprise and the valour of a soldier. In conversation, there were few men who so gained upon his hearers, by the point and vivacity of his remarks, and the unaffected earnestness and sincerity of his whole demeanour. But in public debate he was by no means equal to many who were far his inferiors in moral and intellectual qualifications. There hung about him a bashfulness which he could not shake off, and which gave him somewhat the appearance of a woman in male attire, making an awkward effort to perform some feat of strength or of activity. Still, his indomitable energy and perseverance gave him a kind of forty-horse power amongst the Irish revolutionists; and he might be truly described as the great political steam-engine, without the aid of which nothing important was to be effected.[5]

We cannot be sure, but this gives the impression of a man who both knew Tone and enjoyed his company. It is certainly an unforgettable vignette.

Old Orangeman dutifully related the standard theological critiques of Roman Catholicism, complete with scriptural chapter and verse. There was, however, a discreet distancing from the wilder Protestant claims. He wrote, for example, of the Order's earliest days that:

> it was *believed* by Protestants that Roman Catholics would not keep faith with heretics. It was *believed* that the tenets of their church were intolerant and persecuting, and that they only wanted opportunity in order to carry them fully into effect. This persuasion, no doubt, had its influence on those by whom the original regulations of the Orange Institution were drawn up, and, *if well founded*, entirely justifies their exclusion of a body of men who never could sympathise with the feelings of Orangemen, and who could only give the evidence of their treachery to one system as a proof of their fidelity to the other.[6]

Montanus was certainly prepared to argue that a right-reading on Roman Catholic doctrine could support the gravest charges against it, but he was equally willing to admit that the contemporary chorus of Catholic disavowal of any intent to persecute, from both clergy and laity, was genuinely meant. He countered this by an intriguing socio-psychological riposte. The structure of Catholic belief was such that it created a bent in the Catholic mind that only required a crisis for it to erupt into persecutory violence. 'It may not be seen or felt in times of quiet... But let different circumstances present themselves, let excitement prevail... then it will be seen what the principles are by which [Catholics] are in reality actuated.'[7] Roman Catholicism, from this point of view, was a kind of mental infection, sometimes in remission, sometimes flaring up.

Old Orangeman condemned Roman Catholicism primarily for its psychological impact on its followers. While Protestantism appealed to and supported 'advanced human nature,' as he believed, Catholicism hedged the mind about with obfuscation and ignorance. In particular, two aspects of Catholicism acted to corrupt the morals of the laity. First, the Catholic doctrine of 'exclusive salvation' meant that anyone outside the church was condemned as a heretic undeserving of sincerity or respect. Second, the sacrament of confession implied that Catholics could freely sin in the expectation that a ritual of contrition would expunge them any moral taint or ethical responsibility. Old Orangeman was less concerned with whether these beliefs accurately accorded with the doctrine of the Roman Catholic Church (they did not) than with their prevalence amongst the Catholic peasantry at large. It was to this psychological demoralisation, rather than the more obvious reactions to a deeply iniquitous land system and the oppressions of national and sectarian discrimination, that Montanus attributed the notorious restiveness of the Irish Catholic peasantry. He pointed to the existence of numerous peasant secret societies, grouped under the popular label of the *buachaillí* or 'boys', whose activities ranged from threatening letters sent to landlords and their agents, through violent attack on those who took over the farms of evicted tenants, to outright insurrectionism:

> No man can deny the dreadful system of crime at present in operation in this country; no man can deny that both life and property are fearfully insecure. Now, there are very few who have contemplated the characters of our peasantry without perceiving in them much to commend — much to win upon their love and admiration. They are proverbially a kind-hearted and affectionate people, with as little of gall or of bitterness in their composition as is to be found in any peasantry upon the face of the earth. How, then, are we to account for the strong contrast to all this which is exhibited in their conduct? how are we to account for the fact, that not only are they given to the perpetration of enormous crime, but that these crimes are perpetrated with a remorseless barbarity by which the North American savages are outdone, and which could only be paralleled by the familiars of the Inquisition? Manifestly only by supposing that they are under the influence of a creed by

> which the natural conscience is seared as with a red-hot iron, and which imposes upon them the persuasion that oaths are perjuries where their observance would be prejudicial to the church, and that humanity is weakness when it would interpose any obstacles to the extirpation of those who are believed to be the enemies of true religion. This is the only mode of accounting for the present perverted state both of feeling and principle in Ireland. The nature of the people has been changed by their creed; it has been transmuted from good into evil.[8]

We find Montanus, therefore, drawing a certain distance from the more bigoted claims of Protestant controversialists, even as he quoted them with approval, but his caveats were not made with any liberal intent. His 'culturalist' argument led inexorably to the conclusion that the Catholic unconsciousness was irreformable and irredeemable:

> When I hear Roman Catholics disclaim the persecuting tenets of their church, although I distrust, I do not disbelieve them. On the contrary, I entertain no doubt that they are, at the time, perfectly sincere in their asseverations. … [But has not] the spirit of his religion … by various decrees, and precepts and examples … encouraged every project for the humbling of heretics and the exaltation of the church, no matter how opposed to justice and humanity? Now, this is precisely the case of the Roman Catholics of Ireland. … Such are the precepts of their religion; and on every one occasion where their prejudices were inflamed and their passions excited, their conduct has been uniformly conformable thereto.[9]

Old Orangeman, and indeed much of Irish and British Protestantism at large in this period, certainly accepted the idea that Catholic Ireland had a radically distinct 'subaltern epistemology', as it might now be phrased, but he saw this not in any 'decolonising' frame, but as an unanswerable justification for Protestant Ascendancy.

Even as Montanus found the worst of Catholic brutality in the common mass, he had no problem acknowledging that the Orange Order itself 'had its origin amongst the humblest of the peasantry'.[10] Certainly this was a class inoculated by its religion, but Old Orangeman was far from being complacent. The first benefit of the Orange Order was that it protected the Protestant lower orders from those innate democratic instincts particular to their class position that might otherwise seek to challenge the good order of a civilised society. Unlike the *buachaillí*, the Orange brethren from the very beginning had looked to their social superiors for leadership and direction and with humble striving overcame the snobbery and distrust of their gentry. As it consolidated, the Orange Order became an invaluable medium for class collaboration and socially disciplining plebeian Protestants. As Old Orangeman said with much satisfaction, 'the very humblest of its members felt proud of a bond of connection by which they were brought into brotherly union with the very highest and the noblest in the land; and there was a natural anxiety on their part not to prove unworthy of such a distinction.'[11] Montanus, therefore, could recommend the Orange Order as a model of pan-class counter-revolutionary organisation in an era of rising democracy.

It is important to remember that British and Irish conservatives at this time were deeply averse to popular mobilisation even in their own cause. They feared and resented common people organising in 'clubs' and intruding into the political sphere.[12] It was precisely the 'club government' of the Jacobins and *sans culottes* that had led to anarchy and Terror in the French Revolution. Popular club agitation for democratic reform, in the form of the Political Unions, had brought Britain perilously close to revolution in 1831 and 1832. It was a settled conservative conviction, amply theorised by Edmund Burke, that the 'swinish multitude' had no right or ability to interfere in the serious business of policy and governance. Affairs of State were a matter reserved for the so-called 'representatives' of the nation, drawn from the propertied and particularly the landed classes, who were not delegates of popular opinion, but protectors of the kingdom's interest. This was the view of all Tories, almost all Whigs, and indeed the *DUM*'s editors.[13]

Old Orangeman, however, was a man of the eighteenth-century, who well remembered the glory days of that great, and armed, political union, the Irish Volunteers. He refused to see popular rallying in the conservative cause as only an emergency expedient, to be abandoned as soon as an imminent threat to the constitutional order fell away. In the Letters he made the case for a permanent popular mobilisation behind the conservative cause as an imperative in the new conditions of an increasingly class-conscious society. It was clear that Old Orangeman genuinely feared the potential for a democratic ideology to unite the masses in opposition to the elites. He warned that there was 'a *natural* tendency' for the great mass of poor people to gravitate towards 'such combinations as are unconstitutional'. Attachment to law, order and social hierarchy, he warned, 'are *not* feelings or sentiments to which men are *naturally* prone'. The Orange Order was a necessary bulwark precisely because 'Conservative feelings and principles are, as it were, hot-bed plants which require to be cherished' while radical opinions 'resemble weeds which require to be repressed.'[14] The Orange Order, therefore, was vital as a bulwark against both British Radicalism and Irish Papism, strengthening conservativism by giving it an imposing material strength.[15] Its ability to speak to the emotions of the common people, and to give them a sense of their strength, power and importance in the State, was a necessity for the counter-revolutionary cause. Old Orangeman looked back, therefore, to the great public agitations of the eighteenth-century, but he also looked forward to the ideologies and forms of militant popular conservatism in the modern era, to the populist radical-right, even to fascism. The great interest of these Letters is that they provide us with an analytical history of the Orange Order in its first phase from the perspective of the new and vigilant 'reactionary democracy'.

ORIGINS OF THE ORANGE ORDER

'Old Orangeman', of course, was not trying to write an objective history and he could assume a good deal of prior knowledge on the part of his contemporary readers. In this edition, the Letters have been annotated for sake of clarity, but it will be as well to provide an overview here of the Order's history in these years.

Montanus was writing at an apposite time for taking stock of the Order's history, for it seemed to be coming to a definitive end. His story was one of 'rise and fall'. The origins of the Orange Order were to be found in the County of Armagh. With a population divided in roughly equal portions between Church of Ireland, Presbyterian and Catholic, this was a zone of sectarian friction but it was by no means 'backward'. Armagh was a vigorous centre of flax growing, bleaching and fine-cloth linen manufacture, 'a hot-bed for cash for the industrious farmer and weaver.'[16] In the south of the county was a district known as the Upper Fews which had long been notorious for Catholic-Jacobite banditry. It was in part to supress this that landlords had sponsored colonisation by linen-working Protestants from other parts of Ulster.[17] Combats between Catholic 'natives' and Protestant 'settlers' were frequent. Class and denominational tensions also divided the Protestant community in the county, however. Presbyterian peasants organised as 'Steelboys' were principally a phenomenon of Counties Down and Antrim, but overlapped into Armagh They frequently rioted against onerous landlords between 1769 and 1772. As arrests and emigration shattered Steelboy ranks, its veterans took to 'frequently and wantonly' insulting Catholics at funerals and religious gatherings.[18]

Protestant Volunteer companies, which had first formed in Belfast in March 1778, ostensibly to support the army in warding off French invasion, quickly spread across Ulster and Ireland. They would prove to be the seed-bed both for militant nationalism and, in time, the Orange Order. The Volunteers acted as the armed wing of the 'Patriot' party in the Irish Parliament, led by Henry Grattan, and it was their threat of force which in 1782 wrested from Britain a recognition that the Dublin Parliament was the sole legislative authority for Ireland. The Volunteers were unenthusiastic about arming the boys of Armagh and the Protestant peasantry there, who saw themselves as a kind of frontier garrison, seethed.[19] At the conclusion of the American War in 1783, which ended the invasion scare, an attempt was made to call in Volunteer arms. A small number of Catholics who had managed to join the Volunteers were late in returning theirs and Armagh Protestants, already smarting with resentment, began raiding their homes to seize them. A pre-existing Protestant faction, largely Presbyterian and some at least trained in the Volunteers, became the focus for this activity and, on 4 July 1784, the 'Peep o'Day Boys' Protestant peasant movement was formed at Markethill, at the foot of the Fews. Catholic factionists in response reorganised as Defenders.[20] By 1789, according to a Protestant clergyman, 'the infernal rancor of relig[ious] Party' in County Armagh was threatening to 'untye all the Bands by which Society is held together'.[21] These 'party fights' between Peep o'Day Boys and Defenders were actually rather restrained in most cases and there were few fatalities.[22] On 19 January 1791, however, a torch-bearing squad of Defenders raided a home at the centre of a Protestant colony that had recently been planted at Forkhill within the Fews. There they mutilated the hands and tongues of Alexander Barclay and his wife, in protest at their attempts to educate local Catholic children into Protestantism.[23] The outrage was long remembered by Armagh Protestants, and was to become part of Orange lore.[24]

It does seem to have ended the Armagh cycle of fighting, however, and until 1795 the disorders there simmered down into 'personal enmities'.[25]

The Defenders, meanwhile, spread out from Ulster into Connacht and Leinster, becoming a general body of Catholic peasant assertion. Radicalised by the French Revolution, they developed an increasingly assertive if always rather indeterminate ideology of republicanism and separatism. By 1792, they had effectively re-founded as a revolutionary movement of the Catholic lower class. It was 'the poor who formed the fraternity' and, relying upon a system of passwords and catechisms, they declared their determination to 'stand by each other'.[26] In the summer and autumn of 1792, the Defenders drew together with the United Irishmen, an urban movement of Presbyterians in the North and middle-class Catholics and Protestants in the South, who, in their frustration at the corruptions of the Irish Parliament and British-appointed Government, were rapidly evolving towards supporting an outright revolution to establish an independent and democratic Irish republic. In the spring and summer of 1793, Defender resistance to conscription into the Government's militia approached the dimensions of outright rebellion. By 1795, they had fully coalesced with the United Irish movement, comprising its peasant-rank-and-file at least outside the Ulster Protestant heartland, and were preparing for a concerted rebellion, with or without French aid. The Government reported that, 'having established a brotherhood almost as sacredly kept as freemasonry, the Defenders act in different quarters with a degree of consistence much more formidable than greater accidental insurrections'.[27]

It was in these circumstances that the troubles in Armagh once again erupted. On 12 July 1795, following an inflammatory anti-Papist sermon by Church of Ireland Rector George Mansell in Portadown, local Protestants went on the rampage, burning Catholic homes and beating to death two men they found cutting turf. The Defenders, anxious to avenge the outbreak, issued a challenge to the 'Protestant Boys', who agreed to meet them near Portadown. The Defenders took up position on the hill of Faughart, while the Protestant Boys, led by Joseph Atkinson, a local landlord, occupied a strong defensive position on The Diamond, a crossroads and cluster of houses. The latter were well-armed with old Volunteer firearms supplemented by contributions from local squires. Conflict was almost avoided by negotiation but when, on 21 September, new Defender contingents arrived from the uplands beyond Ballygawley and from the Keady district, about 300 of them rushed the Protestant position, only to be driven off by concerted fire. It was said that they left about 30 dead on the field, though the body-count of famous Orange victories tended to grow in the retelling. That evening, during Protestant celebrations in the town of Loughgall, and fearing retaliation, the Orange Society was formed at the home of James Sloan, an innkeeper.[28]

The Orangemen were distinct from the Peep o'Day Boys in that they were made up primarily of Church of Ireland adherents rather than Presbyterians and because from the outset they declared their willingness to submit to the leadership of the local Anglican gentry.[29] Nonetheless, they were a movement very much from below. R. M. Sibbett writes that, 'almost all engaged in it belonged to the humbler classes – weavers and small farmers' and for some time the gentry cautiously 'stood aloof'.[30] The earliest surviving rule of the Armagh Orange organisation was clearly composed by men of elementary education and considerable organisational capacity. Rule 5 stated that 'that no Roman Catholic can be admitted to our Society by any mains [sic]', forever a defining feature of the Orange Order.[31] Active patronage came at first not from gentry but the larger farmers and linen dealers of the county, who urged a 'driving from this quarter of the Country of its entire Roman Catholic population.'[32] Before long, as local magistrates alerted the country, Orangemen were waging a 'persecution accompanied with all the circumstances of ferocious cruelty' against Catholic peasants, banishing them from Armagh and seizing their property.[33] Some 4,000 Catholics, about 700 families, were forced west into Connacht, while Presbyterians suspected of United Irish sympathies were driven off north to Belfast.[34] Defenders scrambled to resist and before long 'almost every man of the lower orders of every sect was implicated in offences against the law' in Armagh county.[35] Quelling their initial distaste, the local magistrates swung behind the Orangemen as a counterweight to subversive Defenderism.[36]

As the 'Armagh Outrages' petered out, important local gentry, led by the Atkinsons, Blackers, Verners, Knoxes and Warings, began to offer explicit support and leadership to the Orange peasantry. The first Orange 'Twelfth' demonstration took place on 12 July 1796, several thousand strong. By this time there were 90 lodges of the Order. They were still dwarfed by the United Irishmen, who enrolled a 121,000 across Ireland, about 60 per cent of them in the northern counties of Down, Antrim, Derry, and in parts of Donegal and Tyrone.[37] In the counties of Armagh, Cavan, Monaghan, Fermanagh, and part of Tyrone, however, the Anglican Orange peasantry now sustained a powerful counter-organisation. Seeing their potential, the Government began to lend its support and with its indulgence the Orange organisation spread widely. By the middle of 1797, R. M. Sibbert writes, there were at least 315 Orange lodges in existence. Having acquired the confidence of the local gentry and of the Government, they assumed a bolder attitude. 'The days, or rather the nights, of meeting on hills, behind hedges, at lime-kilns, on bog banks, and in other out-of-the-way spots was now over.'[38] In June 1797, important aristocrats and Government supporters in Dublin formed Lodge No. 176 in Dublin, with the intention of attracting the respectable and asserting control.[39] Even now, however, the Orange peasantry organised as typically rural 'boys', being inducted into the Order 'on the road or hillsides'.[40]

In September 1796, Lord Lieutenant Camden authorised the establishment of the Yeomanry, armed Protestant units recruited and led by gentry. The government opened the doors of the Yeomanry to Orangemen wherever they were to be found, fully aware that that their overt sectarianism antagonised the Catholic peasantry. In March 1797, one Orange landlord, now a Yeomanry commander, outlined his rationale in leading his men to search the Catholic parts of Armagh for arms:

> I have arranged a plan to scour a district full of unregistered arms, and this I do, not so much with a hope to succeed to any extent, as to increase the animosity between Orangemen and the United Irish. Upon that animosity depends the safety of the centre counties of the North.[41]

It was the Orange Yeomanry which 'dragooned' Ulster in the late spring of 1797, freely burning and flogging to uncover United Irishmen arms caches. The Orange Order was given direct support by the military commander in the region, General Gerard Lake, who reviewed the Orangemen's 12 July parade at Lurgan. With the United Irishmen under the cosh, Orange lodges began appearing even in Belfast, the heartland of Presbyterian radicalism. Already the Order was becoming a refuge for repentant United Irishmen anxious to restore their good standing with the winning side. Lord Charlemont, formerly commander of the Volunteers, was informed by a Belfast informant in May 1797 that:

> Your old Ballymascanlon Volunteers, who six months ago were almost all United Irishmen are now complete Orangemen, which is more congenial to their feelings. ... In speaking of this astonishing increase of Orangeism, I forgot to mention the most part wonderful of it, that immense numbers of them are in Belfast.[42]

If Orangeism was already helping to roll back the United Irishmen tide in Ulster, it was fanning the flames of insurrection elsewhere in Ireland. The United Irishmen made much use of the Orange bogey in their recruitment propaganda. This was still of service to a government which was keen to see subversion forced into an untimely rebellion, the better to crush the movement in blood.

When outright rebellion did erupt in 1798, Orangemen were active in its repression, both as Yeomen and as irregularly authorised detachments, but the Order does not seem to have played much of a role in battling the insurgents in its own right. There was no mention of its contribution either in military despatches or the thanks voted by the Irish Parliament.[43] The Yeomanry, usually described as 'Orange' by both supporters and opponents, were heavily implicated in burnings, torture, murder, and other outrages. 'These men have saved the country, they now take the lead in rapine and murder,' General Cornwallis wrote.[44]

As the rebellion collapsed, a steady stream of Ulster Presbyterians advertised their new loyalty by joining the Yeomanry and the Orange Order. Formerly subversive Protestants and Presbyterians were positively welcomed, while Catholics were turned away.[45] The Orange Institution, however, approached a dangerous point of division over the Government's determination to abolish the old Irish Protestant Parliament and force through the 'Union' of Britain and Ireland with a single United Kingdom parliament at Westminster. There is little doubt that the Protestant and anti-Catholic Irish patriotism of most Orangemen was offended, but the Grand Orange Lodge on 5 January 1799 passed a resolution forbidding members from taking sides on the question of legislative union. Nonetheless, on 1 March 1800, 31 Orange Lodges met at the Maze, County Down, to resolve that 'We consider a legislative Union with Great Britain as the inevitable ruin to peace, prosperity and happiness in this kingdom.'[46]

Orange solidarity was restored by a concerted propaganda campaign to highlight insurgent atrocities at Scullabogue and Wexford Bridge during the 1798 rebellion.[47] Old Orangeman gave particular credit to Sir Hardinge Giffard for spreading lurid accounts of loyalist Protestants being massacred and in so doing he persuaded many erstwhile republican Ulster Protestants that they had been 'but blindly erecting a spiritual tyranny, to which, sooner or later, they themselves must fall victims.'[48] Robert Emmet's attempted rebellion of 1803 accelerated the shift towards the Orange Order, as gentry put renewed pressure on their Protestant tenants to join up and officers of the Army and Militia, anxious to shake off suspicion that they were United Irish infiltrators, rushed into the Order in substantial numbers.[49] As the prosperity of the domestic weaving trade entered a prolonged period of crisis between 1800 and 1830, Ulster Protestant emigration increased. Anxious not to lose loyal tenants, Landlords encouraged the formation and growth of Orange societies on their estates.[50] The old 'rebellious and insurrectionary propensity' of the lower orders in Ulster, Sir William Cusack noted in September 1813, was steadily being displaced into sectarianism, 'turbulent, bigoted, riotous and affronting, very saucy … almost proud of transgression'.[51]

ORANGEISM IN FAVOUR

For the next 15 years, Orange connections dominated the Government of Ireland, particularly in the person of William Saurin, Attorney General from 1807 to 1822. While the Tories had not been opposed in principle to the admission of Catholics into Parliament and various governmental roles at the time of the Union, opposition to 'Catholic Emancipation' emerged as a rallying cry for the Tory Government in the years following. The Orange Order were delighted at this continuation of 'Protestant Ascendancy' under the Union, and its members were increasingly inclined to rest easy. Attempts by social elites to gradually demobilise the lower ranks of Orangeism were soon arrested, however.

In 1811, a confrontation between Orangemen and Catholics at Fannet in County Donegal resulted in seven Catholics being put on trial. Even the magistrate had to admit that the evidence against them was weak, and he recommended acquittal. The Orange jury, nonetheless, ignored direction from the bench and found them guilty. Furious Catholics in response established the 'Ribbon society'.[52] In the first instance, this was a league requiring members to provide alibis, whether true or not, for Catholics who found themselves in trouble with the law. The Ribbon association quickly spread across the North and took a shape and form not dissimilar from that of the Defenders. As Old Orangeman put it, just as 'Defenderism at first provoked the Orangemen to combine, Ribbonism now causes them to continue their combination.'[53]

The Ribbon-Orange feud wracked Ulster in these years, with frequent stick-fighting battles if relatively few fatalities. In June 1814, Sir Henry Parnell presented to parliament ten petitions gathered from locations across the north of Ireland lamenting:

> the distracted state of Ireland, in which a faction, calling themselves Orange-men, bound together by a secret, and, as the petitioners conceive, an illegal oath, have disturbed the peace by their riotous and tumultuous proceedings … Their processions, decked with party insignia, and frequently with military arms, on certain stated anniversaries, produce much irritation in the minds of those against whom the insulting show is chiefly directed … These processions have a powerful effect in keeping up a spirit of animosity among neighbours, and perpetuating an organized system of hostility towards all who will not join with them … Such irritating proceedings appear not remotely to portend the horrors of civil war.[54]

The Orangemen were engaged in a process of stamping their authority over territory. As the official historians of the Order put it in 1967:

> When reports of disorder, intimidation, and 'agrarian' crime came in from the South, the northern Protestant refused to allow the slightest self-assertion to the 'other side', lest the same occur in his own neighbourhood. On the 12th of July, and on other occasions, he marched with his lodge behind his regalia (cockade, ribbons, scarf or sash) and armed with his yeoman gun, to show his strength in the places where he thought it would do most good. Where you could 'walk' you were dominant, and the other things followed.[55]

Drumming and music made sure that no-one could simply ignore the Orangemen when they were at 'walk'. George Ensor, a liberal Protestant, complained that 'drummers and fifers … annoy the country from about eight to nearly midnight by their noise and intent'.[56] As might be expected, riotous collisions were frequent. Nonetheless, The Orange Order virtually controlled the magistracy in the north, and Orangemen rarely faced the full wrath of the law. Judge Fletcher, addressing the Grand Jury of County Wexford in 1814, gave his experience:

> I have found that those societies, called Orange Societies, have produced most mischievous effects; and particularly in the North of Ireland. They poison the very fountains of justice; and even some magistrates under their influence, have, in too many instances, violated their duty and their oaths. … Of this I am certain, that so long as those Associations are permitted to act in the lawless manner they do, there will be no tranquillity in this country; and particularly in the North of Ireland There those disturbers of the public peace, who assume the name of Orange Yeomen, frequent the fairs and markets, with arms in their hands under the pretence of self-defence, or of protecting the public peace, but with the lurking view of inviting the attacks from the Ribbonmen, confident that, armed as they are, they must overcome defenceless opponents, and put them down. Murders have been repeatedly perpetrated upon such occasions; and though legal prosecutions have ensued, yet, such have been the baneful consequences of those factious Associations, that under their influence, Petty Juries have declined (upon some occasions)

> to do their duty. These facts have fallen under my own view. … With these Orange Associations, connect all commemorations and processions, producing embittering recollections, and inflicting wounds upon the feelings of others; and I do emphatically state it as my settled opinion, that until those Associations are effectually put down, and the arms taken from their hands, in vain will the North of Ireland expect tranquillity or peace.[57]

Orangemen were able to provoke and fire on Catholic mobs without much concern that they would be held amenable at law. In 1825, Daniel O'Connell gave a succinct account of Orange coat-trailing procedure:

> The Orangemen go to fairs unarmed; certainly the Catholics, many of whom are Ribbonmen, go equally unarmed, but the Orangemen, in general, leave their arms in a depot, about a mile or half-a-mile from the fair. In the evening particularly, a riot is easily excited, and the Ribbonmen are equally willing to commence it with the Orangemen; then the practice has been for the Orangemen to retreat upon their arms, and take their arms and shoot away, and many lives have been lost.[58]

Such occasions were not systematically recorded, but four men were killed at such battles at Kilrea (Londonderry) and near Downpatrick (Down) in 1802, one at Derrygonnelly (Fermanagh) in 1811, five at Ballynahinch (Down), Belfast and Carrowkeel (Sligo) in 1812, at least five in Belfast and Garvagh (Londonderry) in 1813, three at Kilrea and Aughnacloy (Tyrone) in 1818, and one at Ederney (Fermanagh) in 1824.[59] Roadside assaults and murders were unremarkable.[60] This was mostly an Ulster phenomenon. Orangeism was never strong in the south outside Dublin and Bandon in Cork. The level of fatality was not drastic but injuries, sometimes serious, were far more common.

The government was never entirely happy about their reliance upon a 'secret society' to suppress the Catholics. Ministers were perturbed by what they saw as a 'sort of loyal association upon

Jacobin principles' as Lord Buckingham put it.[61] When the Unlawful Oaths (Ireland) Act came into force on 20 June 1810, the Grand Orange Lodge of Ireland had to adopt new rules which omitted the secret articles it had adopted in 1800. From about 1820, the Tory Government in London shifted into a rather more liberal phase. In 1821, Lord Wellesley, personally in favour of Catholic Emancipation, was appointed Lord Lieutenant of Ireland, and he authorised suppression of Orange demonstrations taken to be provocative, such as the decoration in Orange colours of King William III's statue in Dublin. The December 1822 'bottle riot', when the offending item was thrown in a Dublin playhouse at the Lord Lieutenant by Orange supporters amongst the audience, enthused the Orange rank-and-file but forced its leadership into new circumspection.[62] In 1822, and again in 1829, the Commander-in-Chief of the Forces forbade the holding of Orange lodges in any regiment as being 'fraught with injury to the discipline of the army', though to little effect.[63] The continuing spread of Orangeism into Britain and the armed forces provoked the Radical MP Joseph Hume into a long anti-Orange campaign from 1823.

Serious rioting on 12 June 1823 at a fair in Maghera, County Londonderry, between Orangemen and Catholics meant that the Orange Order could not be excluded from the provisions of the Unlawful Oaths Act passed later in that year to supress peasant secret societies such as the Ribbon association and the Rockites. The Orange Order responded by abolishing its oath but requiring members to show that they have taken a legal oath of royal and Protestant supremacy, abjuration or allegiance before a magistrate.[64] During Daniel O'Connell's mass campaign for Catholic Emancipation the Orange Order was somewhat neutered, despite or because of the fact that the Catholic Association committed a portion of its membership fee, the famous 'Catholic rent', to combatting 'Orange oppression'. Nonetheless, it was clear that the Order was still considerable power in the land. The Duke of Cumberland was Grand Master of the Order; Lord Kenyon, Deputy Grand Master in Great Britain; Lord Enniskillen, Deputy Grand Master in Ireland; and two members of Parliament, Henry Maxwell, who sat for Cavan, and Alexander Perceval, who sat for Sligo, were Grand Secretary and Grand Treasurer respectively. Lord Goulburn, Chief Secretary of Ireland between 1821 and 1827, was reputed to be a sworn Orangeman. 'No one could expect that the law against secret societies would be enforced when princes of the blood and Cabinet ministers set an example in disobeying it.'[65]

ORANGE DECLINE

When on 9 March 1825 the government passed its Unlawful Societies (Ireland) Act forbidding 'political confederacies', its primary intention was to suppress the Catholic Association, but the Orange Order was caught in the net too. On 18 March the Orange Order reformed itself as the genteel Loyal and Benevolent Orange Institution of Ireland, with the Earl of Aldborough as Grand Master. It suspended marching and left its rank-and-file largely leaderless.

The Catholic Association met the letter of the proscription law while ignoring its spirit, and in May 1828 Daniel O'Connell dramatically won a by-election that had roused the Catholic nation. The Government realised that Ireland teetered on the brink of revolution but even them dangerously delayed the inevitable concession of Emancipation (eligibility of Catholics for Parliament and state offices). In August 1828, Orange leaders sponsored the formation of Brunswick Constitutional Clubs to preserve 'the integrity of the Protestant Constitution'. This was a front for the Orange Order, but focussed on the social elites rather than the Protestant peasantry. With the lapsing of the Unlawful Societies Act, the Orange Order revived in its own name in

September 1828. It continued to keep its plebeian base on a tight leash. The Grand Lodge of Ireland was heavily stacked: 15 of its 25 members were Anglican clergy.

O'Connell was fearful, nonetheless, that there existed a high risk of a disastrous collision between the Orangemen of Ulster, who 'preserved among them the traditional maxims of discipline and organisation that had so long given them a power far exceeding their proportionate numbers', and the Catholic population led by the Ribbonmen, newly organised to 'an almost military uniformity of movement'.[66] In the autumn of 1828, John Lawless led thousands of Catholic supporters into Ulster, with the aim of marching on Belfast, still at this time a fairly liberal town. Ribbonmen, armed with nothing but sticks, were prominent amongst his followers.[67] At Ballybay in County Monaghan they were met by Orangemen wielding firearms, officered by Samuel Gray, a publican of the town. The army intervened and the Catholics forced into retreat. This 'Thermopylae of Protestant Ireland' immediately entered into Orange legend.[68] Gray continued to dominate his area for many years, forbidding Catholics to overstay Ballybay without a pass. In 1841 he was acquitted of murder by a jury packed with Orangemen and in frustration the police had his son transported for jury-tampering.[69]

In April 1829, the Government finally conceded Catholic Emancipation. O'Connell now hoped that with Protestant Ascendancy fatally weakened he could effect a new compact with chastened Orangeism. He hoped to do this by appealing to the Order's still quite recent anti-Unionism. As O'Connell put it in a private letter:

> My plan is to restore the Irish Parliament with the full assent of Protestants and Presbyterians as well as Catholics. I desire ... salutary restoration without revolution, an Irish parliament, British connexion, one King, two legislatures.[70]

In appealing to Protestants, he seems to have made some head-way. The British political diarist Charles Greville noted of O'Connell on 30 December 1830 that:

> having been throughout the Catholic question the furious enemy of the Orangemen, upon whom he lavished incessant and unmeasured abuse, he has suddenly turned round, and inviting them to join him on the Repeal question, has not only offered them a fraternal embrace … but he has entirely and at once succeeded, and is now as popular or more so with the Protestants (or rather Orangemen) as he was before with the Catholics.[71]

There were, indeed, small signs of progress to this end in Ulster. In November 1830 a large crowds of weavers, labourers and small farmers, comprising 'Orangemen, Catholics and other sects' protested landlords evicting small-holders, demanded 'half rent and no tithe', burned their old battle flags and raised a common tricolour flag incorporating green and orange.[72]

The eruption of the anti-tithe militancy from about 1831, a mass campaign against taxation imposed to support the minority Church of Ireland, allowed the Orange Order to reassert itself. Its Grand Lodge demanded that the Yeomanry, which they dominated, be mobilised to police Catholic demonstrations and to protect tithe-proctors.[73] Lord Lieutenant Anglesey agreed to this in the hope that a stiff injection of sectarian confrontation would break up the nascent peasant alliance between Catholics and Presbyterians 'upon the subject of Rent and Tithe'.[74] The predictable result was a series of Yeomanry fusillades during the subsequent 'Tithe War' (11 were killed at one firing at Newtownbarry in County Wexford in June 1831), and use of the Yeomanry had to be discontinued. In 1832, an act supressing further political processions included Orange walks in its remit.

In the febrile atmosphere of Catholic Emancipation, the Tithe War and the pre-revolutionary crisis in Great Britain over the

Great Reform Act of 1832, the Orange Order was increasingly seen as a dangerously inflammatory provocation. In 1827 the Duke of Cumberland, fifth son of George III, had been elected Grand Master of all the Orange Lodges. He employed as his British organiser Lieutenant-Colonel William Blennerhasset Fairman. During the pre-revolutionary crisis in the run-up to the suffrage-extending Great Reform Act, Fairman attempted to interest the Ultra-Tory gentry of England in the idea of adopting the Orange Order as a mass-based counter-revolutionary shock-force. Joseph Hume, the Radical MP, who had for years been warning that the Orange Order was a standing threat to the parliamentary constitution, succeeded in having a Parliamentary Select Committee appointed in 1835 to inquire. Its evidence and reports 'established beyond doubt what had been general knowledge in Ireland since 1795 – that it, that the Orangemen controlled the Irish yeomanry, had lodges in the army, enjoyed a certain immunity from justice in Ulster and were frequently engaged in civil disturbances.'[75] The Committee reported that there were 1,500 to 1,600 lodges in Ireland alone, containing probably between 150,000 and 160,000 Orangemen, who were accustomed to gather in armed bodies of 10,000, 20,000, and even 30,000 at a time. In Great Britain it was (very wildly) estimated that there were 140,000 members, mostly in urban areas. Between 30 to 40 regiments of the line had their own Orange Lodges.

In 1836, Hume presented to Parliament explosive evidence hinting that the Duke of Cumberland had contemplated a coup d'etat through the agency of the Orange Order. The evidence was not quite conclusive but neither was it disproved. It seems plausible that senior Orange members had been intriguing to place the Duke of Cumberland on the throne as Regent on the excuse that William IV was insane. Princess Victoria, considered dangerously liberal, was to be denied the succession. No absolute proof was found for this startling allegation, but it cast a very dark shade on the Order. When it became clear that the government intended drastic action, the Duke of Cumberland bowed to the inevitable and formally dissolved the Orange lodges on 14 April 1836. Old Orangeman's contribution to the battle to save the Orange Orders seemed to have been for nothing.

ORANGE FUTURE

This was not unexpected. Old Orangeman had ended his essays on a distinctly resigned and valedictory note. 'What an old man, who may be said to have been one of those who "rocked the cradle" of the Institution, could do for it, I have done. I trust it will not be my fate to "follow its hearse".'[76] Within months, the Orange Order appeared to be dead and buried. Old Orangeman was not to know that its long second life stretched ahead.

In 1845, the Party Processions Act banning 'Green' and 'Orange' marching finally lapsed and Lord Roden began re-organising the Orange Brethren under gentry control. Because the Whig Government was concerned that discontent arising from the catastrophic Famine might escalate into revolution, it turned discreetly favourable and even covertly provided the Order with arms.[77] Orange marching was soon as common as ever.[78] It over-reached, however. A clash with Ribbonmen at 'Dolly's Brae' in July 1849, left about four people dead.[79] In the ensuing controversy, the Party Processions Act was re-introduced and three Orange magistrates, including Lord Roden, Deputy Grand Master of the Order, were removed from the bench.[80] The gentry and magistracy withdrew much of its patronage and protection for the Orange Order, which remained practically moribund until the 1860s.[81]

Orangeism, however, was by now deeply entrenched in the Church of Ireland peasantry of Ulster. As Belfast sucked in rural labour, Orange culture became an urban and proletarian phenomenon also. The 'right to march', always most appealing to plebeian Orangemen, was taken up by a small land-owner, William Johnston, in the late 1860s. In 1868, he was elected as a populist and independent MP for South Belfast ahead of a candidate supported by the gentry of the Belfast Grand Lodge.[82] The Order at large was revived by the Fenian threat in the 1860s and the lapsing of the Party Processions Act in 1872. During the mass agrarian agitation of 1880 to 1882, the gentry overcame its hauteur and renewed its patronage for Orangeism as a counter-revolutionary bulwark.[83] When the Liberal Party in Britain came out in favour of Home Rule in 1885, even the hold-out Presbyterian tenant farmers urban bourgeoisie overcame their suspicion of Orangeism as Anglican-dominated and joined the Order in large numbers. It firmly interlocked with the Unionist Party structure in 1905 when the Orange Order became a constituent part of the newly-founded Ulster Unionist Council. During the Third Home Rule Crisis of 1912 to 1914 it proved its worth as a mobilising force for Ulster Protestant militancy.[84]

With the advent of partition in 1921, a largely self-governing Northern Ireland was erected in the six north-eastern counties of Ulster. The Orange Order became, in effect, a part of the devolved state, dispensing patronage, defining public ceremonial and disciplining the political elites. 'Jobs for the boys', it was said, were arranged 'in lodge'.[85] All Stormont Prime Ministers were members of the Orange Order.[86] Northern Ireland could be justly called 'the Orange State'.

Old Orangeman's hope that he was not simply writing the epitaph for the Orange Order had no doubt been rather forlorn, but as it turned out his 'Letters' are an irreplaceable if largely overlooked source on the first generation of an Institution that would profoundly shape the history of the island for decades to come.

Letter From an Old Orangeman

Dublin University Magazine, August, 1835.

In giving insertion to the following letter, we think it right to preface it with a few observations. Upon a very recent occasion we stated fully and unreservedly our own opinions upon the subject of the Orange Institution, and endeavoured to place before the public such information, as to its origin and character, as might vindicate its members from the gross and utterly unfounded calumnies which have been so industriously circulated against them.[1] We had intended to return to the subject, but our correspondent has, for the present, taken it out of our hands. Our readers will, perhaps, perceive, that much of his letter is a repetition of the statements which we put forward in our former article; but we have lived long enough to learn that the constant repetition of falsehood can only be met by the equally industrious exhibition of truth, and it is well that the facts which we urged should be kept constantly before the public eye. There are many opinions incidentally expressed by our correspondent for which we do not wish to be held responsible. But concurring in general with his views, and convinced that anything that keeps up inquiry upon the subject of Orangeism, must be productive of good, we have determined upon publishing his letter. We beg the particular attention of our readers to the extract from the memorial of Wolfe Tone to the French Directory, so completely corroborating our former statement with regard to the early and extensive organization of defenderism and so directly contradicting Mr. O'Connell's sworn testimony before the Lords' Committee in 1825 — when the honorable and learned gentleman stated that the origin of defenderism was subsequent to the establishment of the first Orange Lodge. (See University Magazine for April, 1835. Vol. V. note to page 478.)[2] We gladly avail ourselves of this opportunity, to return our best thanks to Dr. Stuart, the editor of the *Belfast Guardian*, for much valuable information which he supplied to us relative to the early origin of the Institution, and of which, in our former article, we largely availed ourselves.[3] We are also indebted to him for the correction of an unimportant error into which we had fallen. We had used the expression, the village of the Diamond.[4] Our readers will, perhaps, excuse us if we extract the following from the *Guardian* of April, 21st:

> "Now, with much respect for the talents, research, and information evinced by our excellent contemporary, the Editor of the *University Magazine*, we beg leave to inform him and the public that, in common with the historians, Musgrave and Hardy, he is in error when he asserts that the first Orange Lodge was formed in the village of the Diamond, on the 21st of September, 1795. We, by no means, blame him for his mistake, since even Mr. Verner for a considerable time laboured under the same misapprehension. We now take the liberty of stating that no village existed at the DIAMOND in the year 1795; and even at the present moment, the few houses which are to be found there, scarcely merit the name of a hamlet.[5]
>
> *"Secondly, The Orange Lodge, No. I, was the first established in the beautiful village called the DIAN, situated in Lord Caledon's estate, county of Tyrone.[6] It was held in the house of a man named St. John Duff, where its members have their periodical meetings at the present time, but we believe that the name of the now owner of the place is Hooey.[7] The causes which induced the formation of this and other Lodges were as follow:—*
>
> *Previous to the great fight which took place at the Diamond, an*

immense number of Roman Catholics (probably from 8 to 10,000) had assembled from various quarters — some from Pomeroy, some from Ballygawley, some from the mountainous parts of the county Armagh, and some, as has been alleged, we know not how truly, even from Connaught. It was generally believed that the object which these men had in view was to destroy the houses of the Protestant inhabitants of Loughgall and Kilmore, and their vicinities. Under this impression, a number of Protestants assembled, some of whom (probably about thirty-six in number) had been volunteers, and were well disciplined; the remainder, amounting to 6 or 700, were armed with guns, pistols, and other such weapons of offence and defence as they were able to procure.[8] The dreadful conflict betwixt the two opposing parties took place at the Diamond, which position the Protestants defended against the tumultuous host of their assailants with perseverance and vigour. At last, after a protracted combat, the Roman Catholic party were finally discomfited, and fled in utter confusion, leaving a number of their men dead on the field. In the course of the harvest, several others, who had been slain on that memorable day, (21st September, 1795,) were found, as we have been informed, amongst the corn, then in progress of being reaped. A considerable portion of the routed Romanists made their escape into the county of Tyrone, and alarmed the inhabitants of the Dian and other districts in that neighbourhood. In consequence of these events, Mr. Thomas Wilson (as we have reason to believe) assembled a number of his own friends, who met at the house of Mr. James Sloane, of Loughgall, and held a consultation as to the formation of societies, who were to assemble periodically, abide by certain rules and regulations, and act together for mutual protection.[9] Twelve or more lodges were then planned and constituted, and the matter was so arranged, (we believe by lot,) that No. I. was established in the Dian, in the county of Tyrone. The original form for this number, signed by James Sloane, is, we believe, still in existence."

We trust that it is unnecessary for us to reiterate our solemn declaration, that in identifying ourselves with the cause of the Orange Institution, we have done so only because we believe it to be an association based upon the purest principles of Christian charity, an association of which toleration is the charter, and the only object to maintain the integrity of our constitution and the principles of civil and religious liberty. Let it be proved to us that we are deceived in this belief, and we will join in the cry for its suppression. Once more we reprint the fundamental rule of the Institution.

"This is exclusively a PROTESTANT ASSOCIATION — yet detesting an intolerant spirit, it admits no one into its brotherhood who is not well known to be incapable of persecuting, injuring, or upbraiding any one on account of his religious opinions. Its principle is to aid and assist loyal subjects of every persuasion by protecting them from violence and oppression."[10]

FIRST LETTER FROM AN OLD ORANGEMAN

Dublin University Magazine, August, 1835.

TO THE EDITOR OF THE DUBLIN UNIVERSITY MAGAZINE.

SIR — I am now in my eighty-seventh year, and it is not a little matter that could induce me to take up my pen for the purpose of claiming a place in your pages.[11] But these are times when both old and young are called upon to exert themselves for the public good; and if the latter may be best employed in those active labours by which a proper spirit may be excited amongst the people, and measures taken for arresting the career of the demagogue and the incendiary, in their pernicious work of disorganization, I know not how the former may be more usefully or honourably occupied, than in giving the latter, from time to time, the benefit of their observation and experience.[12]

My present remarks shall be confined to the Orange Institution, which is now, I perceive, upon its trial before a Committee of the House of Commons.[13] I am acquainted with that institution since its formation. I was well aware of the necessity out of which it arose. I knew its founders, most of whom were my personal friends; and I have watched its workings; and never, I will venture to say, was an institution so providentially calculated for the preservation of peace and order, or for furnishing an anti-septic to the contagion of those revolutionary principles which were, at the time of its origin, agitating England, convulsing Ireland, and disorganizing Europe.[14] Judge, then, of my surprise and indignation at hearing it denounced in the House of Commons as the "fons and origo" of all our evils.[15] These denunciations proceeded, indeed, from a party, to whose designs it has always been adverse, and who could not, therefore, be expected to give it a good word.[16] But verily, I was almost amused by their audacity. It was something like hearing Abel accused of the murder of Cain![17]

I well remember the state of feeling in this country in 1795.[18] We are told by the poet, that, "When Hecla thunders, Chimborazo raves," as if there was a kind of subterranean communication between the volcanic mountains, by which they were enabled to sympathise with each other in their eruptions.[19] Politically the same effect was produced in this country by the French Revolution. The smouldering fires of discontent were fanned into a flame, and the convulsion in France seemed but the precursor of similar convulsions in Ireland. The combustible materials had been provided in abundance, and the French revolution seemed well calculated to supply the spark that alone seemed necessary to set them in a flame.

It is not to be denied that Protestants were the first movers of those seditious practices, by which this country was at that time disturbed. A great party had been created by the celebrated Mr. Grattan, which pursued peculiarly Irish objects, in a spirit which could not be so fondly cherished without generating anti-Anglican predilections.[20] In the great political conflict which terminated in the establishment of free trade, views were disclosed, and principles were laid down, which could not be consistently pursued or acted upon without bringing the Irish into frequent collisions with the British Parliament; and, the entire independence of the former having been established by the repeal of Poynings' Law, the heady and intemperate spirits by whom it was guided seemed prepared to run a career of violence, which must, if uncontrolled, have ended in the separation of the countries, possibly in the subjugation of the empire.[21]

I am now free to confess, that I was, at that time, one of those who ardently pursued those phantom delusions which possessed the power of drawing from the straight path of political wisdom so much of the worth and the intellect of Ireland. Grattan was the very Prospero of faction.[22] His eloquence possessed a magical charm which must have been felt in order to be understood. He was, in temperament, a Greek, and in bone and muscle a Roman; and if his winged words lacked any thing of the fiery rapidity of the orators of the one school, it was only because they were laden with the solid thought of the orators of the other. Compared, in the different qualities which constitute a great speaker, with several of the eminent men of his day, he must be allowed to have been their inferior. In depth and reach of philosophic thought, he was far, indeed, inferior to Burke; Flood excelled him in classical taste, and Curran vastly his superior in fancy and in pathos.[23] But no one of his great cotemporaries were able to bring so many powers to bear with such intense and unremitting energy upon those public objects which he had resolved to accomplish. He was the most brilliant and indefatigable leader of an opposition which the Irish House of Commons had ever seen, and was able, at any moment, to play an electrical battery of withering sarcasm and fiery logic upon his opponents, by the splendour of which his friends were delighted and cheered, and by the keenness and the vehemence of which his enemies were abashed and confounded. I well remember the feeling with which I rejoiced at that time to enrol myself under his banners; as I was, certainly, most sincerely persuaded, that in aiding him to the utmost of my power in the accomplishment of his great designs, I was doing that which was most directly conducive to the well-being and the prosperity of Ireland.

Protestantism has ever been favourable to freedom. In the north of Ireland, where Presbyterianism prevailed, the people were excited, to the utmost, by the events which were taking place upon the Continent, and to a manifestation of violence similar to that which had overthrown the government of France, nothing seemed wanting but an occasion and leaders.[24] The parliamentary demagogues, whose violence in the House of Commons had so powerfully served to excite a revolutionary spirit in the country, most ostentatiously identified themselves with the ardent spirits out of doors, who had been stimulated by them to the very verge of treason.[25] I do not, myself, believe, that they contemplated, in the first instance, the extremes to which matters were likely to go, when they championed the national cause against the government of the country. But, in all revolutionary movements you cannot agree to go a certain length without being compelled to go further. The seditious spirit which they had excited now began to exercise a mastery over themselves; and while they were unprepared to submit to the requisitions of the more daring revolutionists, they were altogether unable to impose any effectual restraint upon them.

Grattan now but rarely appeared in public.[26] His sympathies would have led him to side with the anarchists, but his prudence kept him aloof from them; and he was only to be seen, occasionally, like Ossian's heroes in the mists of Morven, the apparition of his former self, leaning, as it were, upon the cloud of his fame, and prepared either to drop unnoticed from public life, or to manifest himself in more than his accustomed energy and power, according as the projects of the revolutionists declined or prospered.[27] He was now an historic character, and naturally disdained companionship with the meaner minds which had been quickened, by the ardent spirit of the times, into an ephemeral existence. But his efforts to become altogether disassociated from them were unavailing. They resembled the efforts of a comet to become separated from its tail; and the very utmost which Grattan could accomplish was, to avoid the responsibility of their acts, for no disavowal of their designs could altogether exonerate him from the suspicion of approving of their principles. His position was one of no small difficulty, and he therein displayed quite as much of prudence as of patriotism. Had rebellion been triumphant, he had done nothing which should have provoked the anger of the republican leaders, or forfeited his claim to such honours and distinctions as they could bestow; had it been put down, there was no overt act of his which could have drawn upon him any indignant animadversion from the government of the country.

When Grattan commenced his advocacy of the Roman Catholic claims, there was everything to excite the sympathy of generous and imaginative minds.[28] The Romish party had been completely humbled by the penal laws,[29] and exhibited a character of such a tranquil and uncomplaining endurance, that these laws, which were sufficiently harsh and severe in themselves, seemed doubly so when contrasted with the quiet and inoffensive demeanour of those against whom they were enacted. Popery was only known in this country as an idle and inoffensive superstition, and its priesthood as a race of harmless, unobtrusive ecclesiastics; many of them men of piety, and some of them possessing no mean share of such learning as was then to be obtained in the continental universities.[30] There was about them a certain character of gentility, partly proceeding from birth, partly from breeding, which was very well calculated to procure for them respect and esteem, not alone amongst their own flocks, but even from their Protestant neighbours; and their apparent total estrangement from active politics, or any ostensible interference in public affairs, except for the purpose of tranquillizing any disorderly spirit by which the suspicion of the government of the country might be excited, served to mark them as a race rather to be encouraged than coerced, and by whose friendly and judicious exercise of the influence which they possessed, much might be done for the tranquillity and the prosperity of Ireland.

The power of oppression in generous minds always begets a disposition to redress. While it may be felt that it is good to have a giant's strength, it is also felt that it would be merciless to use it like a giant. The political crimes of the Roman Catholics were matter of history; their humiliating condition was matter of observation, and as *Segnius irritant animos demissa per aures, Quam quæ sunt occulis subjecta fidelibus ["Things heard with the ears move the mind less forcefully than those which are presented to the faithful eyes"]*; so present prostration and present suffering, when exhibited in conjunction with a quiet and uncomplaining demeanour, excited deeper compassion, than traditionary atrocities and treachery provoked resentment; and it is by no means surprising that the ardent and enthusiastic began to espouse a cause, which, to their lively imaginations and susceptible hearts, must have appeared to be the cause of justice and humanity.

I must also bear my impartial testimony to the fact, that the Protestant clergy were not then what they are now.[31] A respectable and respected race, no doubt, they were, but more as gentlemen than as ecclesiastics. The spirit of their high calling was not sufficiently observable, either in their demeanour or their conduct, and nothing seemed farther from their thoughts than that missionary devotedness by which a large and an increasing number of the present clergy are so honourably distinguished. In the pulpits you seldom heard anything better than a good moral discourse, which might be pronounced in any assembly of respectable heathens, without exciting any suspicion of strange doctrine, as it was confined entirely to the enforcement of the cardinal virtues, from motives which put out of sight, if they did not altogether supersede, all the distinguishing peculiarities of the gospel. Of them, indeed, it might be said, by any one whose soul was athirst for the glad tidings which they came rather to cushion than to proclaim – "they have taken away my Lord, and I know not where they have laid him."[32]

And here I need not travel very far out of my way to make an observation upon one of the characteristic differences between true and false religion. In times of comparative moral darkness, such as those of my early life, the deformities of Popery were not particularly visible; neither were men capable of appreciating, as they deserve to be appreciated, the beauties and the excellencies of the Established Church. But, in proportion as knowledge has increased, and men have become cultivated, the former has sunk and the latter has risen in public esteem; and while no plausibility can justify the absurdities of the one, even in the eyes of many of its own votaries, no misrepresentation or disparagement can blind even candid adversaries to the reasonableness and the spirituality of the other. The most enlightened professors of popery now-a-days endeavour to justify their adherence to it by representing it as almost identical both in doctrine and in discipline with the Church of England. Thus the very same light which has rendered the one attractive, has rendered the other repulsive. While the latter has been losing its hold upon the regards of its members, and becoming year after year less and less calculated to command either reverence or respect, the former has been multiplying its claims to admiration and gratitude, and exhibiting itself as, indeed, like "the shining light that shineth more and more unto the perfect day."[33]

If we are told of the men of distinguished abilities who profess the popish religion, I can only say, look to the lives and the conversation of those men, and before any boast is made that they are Roman Catholics, let us be sure that they are Christians. I would also respectfully refer my readers to the powerful temporal motives which must operate in determining the choice of many a latitudinarian in religion, who may be desirous of a seat in the imperial parliament.[34] Suppose Mr. O'Connell or Mr. Sheil declared their conversion to the Established Church, would not such an event instantaneously annihilate their political influence, if it did not, indeed, destroy their political existence.[35] Most undoubtedly the one would no longer rejoice as the representative of Tipperary, nor would the other exult in the Catholic rent; so that, to embrace an evangelical mode of faith would imply, on their parts, an entire renunciation of private interest and political ambition; sacrifices which could alone be expected from the most unfeigned religious sincerity.[36]

Far am I from denying, or even doubting, that many enlightened individuals even still exist, who have reconciled themselves to a belief in the doctrines of the church of Rome; but I am well satisfied that the great majority of those who profess an attachment to them, consist of men who have never taken the trouble to think very seriously upon the subject, and who use religion merely as a cloak for the more effectual attainment of worldly objects.

Let anyone enter the hall of our courts of Law, and find, if he can, amongst the Roman Catholic advocates, who are both numerous and able, any class corresponding to the evangelical members of the Protestant bar. I mean, by the latter, the class that may be represented by the Pennefathers, the Jacksons, the Scotts, the Littons, the Brookes, and others. Let him find any professors of popery so steadfast in their belief, and so strict in their lives, and so observant of the usages of their religion, as these excellent men are in all that is essential to that system to which they have given an enlightened preference, and which their conduct proves that they have embraced with their whole heart.[37]

Why is this? It is not because Roman Catholics are irreligious, but because popery is uncongenial to enlightened intellect; while it is only to the truly cultivated mind that Protestantism can reveal the brightest of its attractions. The confessional is no substitute for throwing open the heart to God, nor can priestly absolution ever produce the answer of a "good conscience."[38] What I now say, I beg to be understood as said in condemnation of popery, not of papists.[39] While the former is so obnoxious to the reproach of being utterly unable to satisfy the demands of advanced human nature, the latter cannot be expected to be very good Christians; and it is greatly to be deplored that so many inducements of a temporal character should now conspire to keep, in the thraldom of a degrading superstition, numbers who would otherwise be well qualified for experiencing and enjoying the delights and the privilege of that "liberty wherewith Christ would make them free."[40] As far as such as these are concerned, the worst effect of popery is, that, without engaging, it preoccupies their minds, and affords them but little opportunity of forming a candid judgment respecting the reasonableness or the spirituality of that "more excellent way" which we maintain to be most in conformity with the Gospel.[41] They are thus mentally detached from one system, without being spiritually attracted towards the other; and between both, often drop into a state of semi-unbelief, in which, if popery have departed from them, it is only that they might be entered and taken possession of by seven other spirits worse than her, so that their last end may be worse than their first.[42] This is the very class of persons from amongst whom we might expect to find patrons of violence, sedition, disorder, misrule; the apologists of perjury, and the panegyrists of murder.[43] And if we are, fortunately, as yet free from any manifestation which should lead us to believe that distinguished Roman Catholics could be induced thus to act or to think, that exemption only proves that men may sometimes be not only better than their creed, but superior to the corrupting influences by which they are surrounded.

In a system where the higher classes were thus left without any suitable moral provision, we may be sure that the lower classes must have been neglected. Popery differs from all other sects in this important particular, that its liturgy is in an unknown tongue.[44] This one peculiarity must be almost totally obstructive of the influences of the Gospel. In all other systems, no matter how erroneous, the scriptures are read, and prayers in conformity with them are recited. But, in the church of Rome, the unlettered portion of the congregation are almost, if not altogether, dependent upon the pantomime that is exhibited before them, for any serious religious impressions; and what is called divine service amongst them is resorted to much more as a tax upon their time, a kind of tribute which they are obliged to pay to the Supreme Being, "their duty," as they call it, than as a wholesome spiritual exercise, in which the blessed truths of Christianity may be applied experimentally for the purification of their moral nature. The priest to them is all in all. Whatever of spiritual light descends upon them comes only as reflected from him; and he is but rarely instructed in that blessed volume which could alone make him "wise unto salvation."[45]

Many of the forms and ceremonies in the church of Rome were, no doubt, originally well intended. They were adopted in accommodation to the low state, in intellect and morals, of the semi-barbarous tribes, for whom religion must have been palpably materialized, before it could be comprehended. And something, no doubt, was gained for Christianity, by thus permitting it to enter, in any shape or upon any terms, into the ritual of those who had been the worshippers of strange Gods; although the leaven that was hid in three measures of meal was not more completely concealed, than were its truth and its spirit obstructed and impaired under the multiplied observances by which it was encumbered.[46]

At the reformation, the spirit of religion burst, as it were, the cerements in which it had lain buried, and appeared in that exalted character in which it was recognized as, indeed, the best gift of God to man. Its efficacy was soon manifested in a rejection of that "will worship" which had, before, supplied its place, and in turning the hearts of the disobedient to the wisdom of the just.[47] Forms and ceremonies were no longer regarded as substitutes for true religion. Protestants were taught, that, whilst they might be useful as aids, they were dangerous as hindrances; and that those who now worshipped God, should worship him "in spirit and in truth."[48] But Roman Catholics still remained spell bound under the fascinations of the church of Rome. Her commands were observed as law, and her authority superseded the Gospel. As the church of Rome had become not merely a religious but a political system, to which "the faithful" were bound to pay implicit deference, so the hostility to which it was exposed on the part of more orthodox believers, served to excite a kind of chivalrous devotion amongst its partizans; and as the crusaders fondly believed that they were purchasing heaven by their deeds of violence and blood, so Roman Catholics were taught to think that the persecution of heretics, and the extermination of heresy would be attended by a no less glorious reward; and many of them believed that their "good works" in this respect would atone for their flagitious disregard of the plainest precepts of the Gospel.[49] "To root out and to destroy" the professors of a pestilent creed, by whom the authority of the Pope was denied, was regarded by many of them, as, in a most peculiar manner, one of those works of charity which must cover a multitude of sins.[50]

It is thus alone that we can account for that peculiar rancour with which the minds of the lower classes of Roman Catholics in Ireland were animated against their Protestant fellow subjects, when any circumstances enabled them to wreak upon them a deadly vengeance. Their natures were unchristened, as it were, by their addiction to a soul-deadening superstition; and the new commandment, "to love one another," had been superseded by that dictum of the Vatican, which taught them, that the most acceptable service which they could perform to God, consisted in persecuting Protestants even to extermination.[51] Christianity is essentially a religion of love; popery is essentially a religion of hate. The sincere professor of the one finds it difficult "to think any evil" of those who differ from him.[52] The sincere professor of the other finds it difficult to think any good of the maintainers of an opposite belief. He is under the conviction that they are wilfully estranged from the only acceptable mode of serving God, and that their perseverance in this deadly error deservedly incurs damnation.[53] His hand is, therefore, ever ready to be lifted up against them, as the enemies of all righteousness. In him, while under this diabolical influence, humanity has no place. Even the dearest ties of kindred are insufficient to appease or to mitigate that insatiable hatred of heretics which he mistakenly cherishes as the love of God. His very piety and benevolence become the fuel of his unholy zeal; until, to use the eloquent language of Curran, "the human heart is charred in the flame of its own vile and paltry passions; black and bloodless; capable only of catching and communicating that destructive fire by which it consumes, and is itself consumed."[54]

Now, it was to guard against the frequent atrocities to which isolated and defenceless Protestants were exposed, that the Orange system was called into existence. It arose entirely out of the necessities of their condition, and was intended solely as a protection against the combined though desultory system of outrage to which they must have otherwise fallen unpitied victims. When alone on the road side, or when unsupported at fairs or markets, they were often overpowered by numbers, who, no matter how they might be divided in other respects, were united against Protestants, and rejoiced together in the shedding of their blood. It was some time before Protestants could believe this. It was too abhorrent to all their notions to be easily credited. When repeated experience convinced them that there was arrayed against their lives a combination of bigotry and hatred that would never rest while one of them remained, they saw the necessity of associating for self-defence, and concerting the best means of averting or withstanding the coming dangers.

It is not necessary to inform your readers, that from an early period of the last century, Ireland was disturbed by various illegal combinations, which appeared, at different times, under various denominations, as Peep o'Days Boys, defenders, white-boys, &c. &c. whose conflicts certainly partook of a sectarian character; and what would otherwise have been mere party feuds were deepened and embittered by rancorous religious and political differences. The Roman Catholics regarded the Protestants as an accursed race, obnoxious as heretics, to temporal punishment in this world, and to eternal punishment in the world to come. The Protestants regarded them as the professors of a persecuting creed, one of whose tenets enjoined perfidy as a duty, when it might serve the interests of their church, while another proclaimed the uncharitable dogma, that for heretics there was no salvation. It is not, therefore, surprising, that those ordinary wounds and bruises, which, in a more natural state of things, the "vis medicatrix" of the political system would have so speedily cicatrized, should have been gangrened into corroding ulcers, which, even if they had not been aggravated by the empiricism of the quack, would have almost defied the utmost skill of the physician.[55]

One thing is certain. The combinations on the part of the Protestants were strictly defensive; they were, also, desultory and local, while those of their adversaries were extensive and organized. Another thing is equally certain, namely, that while the clergy of the former were totally unconnected with their proceedings, and openly condemned them, as far as they were contrary to law, or marked by any spirit of uncharitableness, the clergy of the latter were in many instances the secret fomenters of the strife; and in some instances so manifestly the accomplices of the disturbers as to render themselves obnoxious to the penalties of the law.

Of the spirit which then animated the Roman Catholic peasantry some idea may be formed from the following extract, for the clear understanding of which it is necessary to premise a few words. In the year 1737, Richard Jackson, Esq. of Forkhill, died, having demised his estate for charitable purposes; and having directed that his demesne should be colonized by Protestants, and that four schoolmasters should be employed for the purpose of teaching indiscriminately children of every religious persuasion. In 1789, the trustees obtained from the Irish Parliament an act of incorporation, and proceeded to act according to the terms of the will; but they immediately experienced the utmost opposition.

The Roman Catholics openly declared, that they would not suffer the establishment of Protestants to take place, and made repeated attempts upon the life of the rector of Forkhill, the Rev. Edward Hudson. Not to detain the reader by detailing the various modes of annoyance that were resorted to, and by which the efforts of the trustees were impeded, I shall confine myself to the single statement which is given below, which is taken from a report made by the trustees to the Bishop of Dromore, and which bears date February, 1791. A more harrowing recital never was made, and the facts have never been disputed. Not even the bloodiest scenes in revolutionary France can rival it in ruthless and deliberate atrocity:

> "On Friday evening, at seven o'clock, a number of villains assembled at the house of Alexander Barclay, one of the schoolmasters of the parish of Forkhill, near Dundalk, appointed by the trustees of the late Richard Jackson's charities, to instruct, indiscriminately, the children of the poor of the said parish. They appeared at the door; he inquired who they were, and one man of the name of Terence Byrne, his neighbour, whose voice he well knew, and had before, at different times, admitted on knowing his voice, told him it was he was there; he opened the door, and a number of men rushed in, threw him on his face, and three of them stood on him, and stabbed him repeatedly. They then put a cord about his neck, which they tightened so as to force out his tongue, part of which, as far as they could reach, they cut off. They then cut off the four fingers and thumb of his right hand, and left him on the floor, and proceeded to use his wife in the same manner. To add to their barbarity they cut out her tongue, and cut off her four fingers and thumb with a blunt weapon, which operation took them about ten minutes, one or two of them holding up her arms while they committed this inhuman action. They then battered and beat her in a dreadful manner. Her brother, a boy about thirteen years of age, had come from Armagh that morning to see her. They cut out his tongue, and cut off the calf of his leg, and left them all three in that situation.

> "No reason can be assigned for this most inhuman transaction. The man was a Protestant, a peaceable and decent man; he taught above thirty of their children GRATIS, being allowed a salary by the trustees for forty more. ASKED THEM WHETHER HE HAD EVER OFFENDED THEM? THEY SAID NOT; BUT THAT WAS THE BEGINNING OF WHAT HE AND THOSE LIKE HIM SHOULD SUFFER."
>
> Shocking as this account is to human nature, it is publicly exulted at in the parish; and no person seems to think that any punishment will follow the commission of this most atrocious wickedness. So far were they from wishing to conceal it, that they proceeded on the road with torches, publicly, and in defiance of everybody. There is every reason to dread the most alarming consequences from the effects of this transaction. The Protestants are everywhere in the greatest terror, and, unless government affords them assistance must leave the country; as this recent instance of inhumanity, and the threatenings thrown out against them, leave no doubt upon their minds what the intentions must be against them. The man and the boy can speak a little; the woman cannot; fortunately they are all likely to die, as, if they live, they are incapable of earning their subsistence. Terence Byrne has fled."

Such was the spirit by which, in that part of the country, the Roman Catholic peasantry were at that time animated. Is it, therefore, to be wondered at, that the Protestants combined for self-defence?[56] Their adversaries had at this time become extensively organized.[57] They had invented a system of signs and pass-words by which they might become known to each other; a fact which, if it arose out of necessity, in itself establishes the extent of the organization; for it could only have been necessary when the confederates became so widely spread, that the ordinary means of knowledge, by personal intercourse, must be, to a considerable degree, precluded. They were also under the obligation of an oath, which bound them to an unrelenting hatred of heretics, and to an unceasing endeavour for their extirpation, and for the reestablishment of the Roman Catholic religion.

As yet, the combination on the part of the Protestants was without any organization. It was extremely confined in its extent, and directed solely against the aggressions to which they were exposed; and by which, if not resisted with an energy somewhat from the ordinary operation of the law, more prompt than could be expected they must have been rooted out of the land. But it was soon found that the secret meetings, the signs and the pass-words of their enemies gave them a great advantage; and that, unless they adopted a similar mode of being united to, and of knowing each other, they could not maintain their ground.

I well remember the frightful state of things that now prevailed in Ulster. On the one hand, there was a dense mass of organized Roman Catholics, who already felt their strength, and who were united both by the prejudices of a sect, and the principles of a party, into a confederacy, having for its object the extirpation of heresy, and the liberation of Ireland. On the other hand, there were the Protestant peasants and farmers, not bound together in any system of association — unsupported, if not discountenanced by their own gentry, amongst whom revolutionary principles very extensively prevailed, and exposed, both by night and day, to outrages against which the laws of the land afforded but a weak protection. I cannot look back upon what I then witnessed without emotions which I shall not attempt to describe. Verily, the days of the devoted Protestants seemed to be numbered. They could not rise up, or they could not lie down; they could not walk out, or they could not sit at the fire-side, without being haunted by apprehensions of the same spirit of merciless outrage to which the poor family at Fork Hill had fallen victims. Their doors and windows were barricaded during the night, as though they were momently in expectation of assault; and they deemed themselves fortunate if they rose from their beds without suffering injury in life or limb, from the shots which were frequently fired through any unguarded aperture, and which were often attended with the most afflicting consequences.

In the open field they might have been a match for their ferocious assailants; and, when waylaid and overpowered by numbers, they often reproached them with their dastardly conduct, and called upon them, if indeed they were men and not assassins, to decide their differences in fair and manly conflict. For this the Protestants would have been both prepared and thankful. But their habits had altogether unfitted them for the cowardly, skulking, murderous, savage, mode of warfare, which their adversaries loved to practise, and to which they had become so habituated, that any other would then have seemed contrary to their nature.

Nor was it long before the Protestants had the opportunity which they longed for. About six miles from the town of Armagh, is situated the townland of the Diamond.[58] This was now destined to be the scene of a conflict which is still remembered by the Protestants with pride, and by their adversaries with terror and resentment. The harassing annoyance to which they had been exposed had kept the Protestants of the neighbourhood in an unusual state of activity and excitement, and this necessitated the assembling, in larger masses, of the Roman Catholics, whose organization gave them a facility of accumulating their forces in a manner by which they imagined their disorganized antagonists must be speedily overpowered. I cannot now venture to give any exact account of the numbers assembled on both sides, but I am within limits when I say that they amounted to several thousands. It is strange that matters should have been suffered to proceed to such a formidable height, when the differences could now only be adjusted by a large effusion of human blood; but I believe the magistrates and the ruling powers were themselves wearied by the perpetual bickerings that were every day occurring, and judged it not inexpedient to suffer the whole of the differences between the hostile parties to be brought at once to a conclusion in a decisive conflict. Whatever the cause was, they interfered not to interpose any obstacles to the battle that was now about to be fought. The best men on both sides grappled in the deadly strife, and dire was the rage, and dauntless the determination, with which the murderous volleys were interchanged, until the unflinching Protestants had the satisfaction of seeing their enemies fly before them, and yield them no inglorious victory.

The Roman Catholics fought well. It was not without much reason that they relied on their numbers, and their combinations, and also on the vast resources which the extensive spread of defenderism had placed at their disposal; and this very confidence may have contributed to their overthrow. The Protestants clearly saw that if now defeated they were altogether undone; and the exertions which they made were worthy of men whose all was at stake, and in whose resolution and constancy was placed their only chance of safety. At one period of the engagement they were pressed very sore, and there seemed but little hope that the scales of victory would incline in their favour. Their ammunition was almost exhausted, while the Roman Catholics were still abundantly supplied. In this strait, two men rode rapidly into the town of Moy, and were approaching the house of a Roman Catholic who sold gunpowder. Seeing them approach, and guessing their object, he hastily closed his door in their faces. But they were not to be disappointed. Necessity, they thought, had no law, and they immediately seized a smith's sledge, and lost not a moment in breaking in the door. This done, the gunpowder was easily provided, but the Protestants left not the shop without leaving the price of it upon the counter. They returned rejoicing to their companions in the field, who were re-inspirited by this seasonable supply, and enabled by it to resume the attack with so much spirit and vigour that their opponents were soon seen to fly in all directions.

A truce was now established, by the mediation of the Roman Catholic priest, on the one side, and on the other by Mr. Joseph Atkinson, who is still alive to tell the story.[59] All that the victorious party stipulated for was, that they should, for the future, be unmolested; that there should be a complete discontinuance of the system of unmanly and treacherous hostility by which they had suffered so much; they on their parts engaging, that, provided this agreement was cordially entered into and faithfully performed, they would, as far as in them lay, live peaceably with all men.

Thus, there was at length afforded some reasonable prospect that internal peace would soon be restored to distracted Ireland. It was, however, but of short continuance. Atkinson could not altogether forego some misgivings respecting the good faith with which the conditions agreed on would be observed by the Roman Catholics, and he warned a few of his followers (to the number, I believe, of twelve or fifteen,) not immediately to return to their homes, but to remain with him for the purpose of seeing that all was as it should be, and to be ready, if occasion required, to rally their friends and renew the combat. It was not long before his precautions were fully justified by the event. The now scattered and confiding Protestants were suddenly attacked by above seven hundred men, who came from the direction of Keady, a distance of about eighteen miles, and commenced their horrid work of devastation with the eager and delighted alacrity with which North American savages carry fire and the sword amongst their sleeping victims. But, although taken by surprise, the Protestants were not disheartened. At the summons of their indefatigable leader they again came in great numbers into the field. The combat was renewed. On the one side was the fury of fresh and vigorous assailants, who enjoyed all the advantages of taking their adversaries unawares, and who hoped, by one decisive overthrow, to extinguish them for ever. On the other there was the indignant ardour of men who felt that they had been most treacherously dealt with — that their generous clemency had been most foully abused — and that, if now overcome, they could entertain no hope of mercy. They, therefore, put forth all their energies and were again victorious. They had the satisfaction of seeing their enemies a second time routed, and flying from the field. And the day on which this memorable event took place, has obtained in the north of Ireland, the significant appellation of "running Monday."

No truce was now made. Protestants felt that they had an enemy to deal with who was not to be trusted, and they had no idea of risking a second time, by hollow negotiation, the loss of the advantages which they had gained in the field. But their first thoughts were not of vengeance. On that important day the Orange Institution was founded. The first lodge was formed on the field of battle, as the commencement of an association which was intended to be strictly defensive. They saw the advantage possessed by their enemies, by means of the union and the organization that prevailed amongst them, and they determined to be no longer wanting to themselves. A system of signs and pass-words was resolved upon, that those who were now knit together, by the endearing bond of brotherhood, and who were determined to stand or fall together, might know each other, when occasion required. A solemn act of thanksgiving to Almighty God was offered up for their recent deliverance, and it was resolved that every meeting of the association should commence and conclude with prayer. It would be well if it could be added that no acts of retaliatory outrage followed the defeat of their perfidious enemies. But, that unlettered peasants should be altogether oblivious of the broken faith of Roman Catholics, in seeking to surprise them when they were unprepared; that they should entertain no resentment for the treachery by which their generous confidence had been requited, and which was so near terminating in their extermination, that they should have no fears of living in the neighbourhood of those who so clearly demonstrated that they could not be trusted, were too much to expect from human nature. I do not justify what followed; but, in the circumstances in which the Protestants were placed, it was but too natural. Several Roman Catholic families were compelled to remove from their habitations and to seek a settlement elsewhere.

Then it was that some of the more violent, provoked by treachery, and flushed by conquest, raised the cry of "to hell, or to Connaught."[60] I do not believe it was directed against Roman Catholics generally, but against those whose conduct on the late occasion proved them capable of anything, and who were believed by the Protestants to have been sworn "to wade knee deep in Protestant blood."[61]

Such was the origin of the Orange Institution; it arose from the pressure of strong necessity. The evil which threatened the Protestants, and which never before was so imminent, could have been averted by no public combination. It required a concentration of energy and power somewhat similar to that by which they were assailed, to enable them to make any effectual resistance; and it was to attain that they associated under circumstances so calculated to inspire them with a sense of their peril, and to make them feel that, while in disconnection they were exposed and weak, in union and combination they were irresistible. Nor is it a little remarkable that the name of our great deliverer, William the Third, was that which they chose as their rallying word and their signal.[62] They did not adopt the name of the field whereon the recent battle was fought and won, and call their body the Diamond Association, although such an appellation would be by no means inappropriate, and would seem to have been sufficiently inviting; but it would have localized what they intended to be general; and it would have seemed to refer to a private feud, which concerned only themselves, rather than to that hatred of their name and race which equally contemplated the destruction of the Protestants of Ireland. Therefore it was that they called their body the loyal Orange Association; and it was because subsequent events too surely justified their suspicions, and served to arouse the jealousy of even the most unsuspecting of their brethren, that their institution rapidly took root, and spread itself through the length and the breadth of the land.

It is but right to mention, in justice to the Orangemen, that most of the individuals, who were driven out of their habitations, were persons some of whom were under ejectment according to a regular process of law; over others of whom heavy prosecutions impended, which would, in all probability, have terminated in the forfeiture of their lives; and others of whom are known to have withdrawn from the country, in the hope of being able to procure more desirable settlements elsewhere.[63] If these three classes were subtracted from the number of those who were then visited for their treachery with this summary infliction, the amount of injury which then could be fairly complained of, would be found to be by no means so considerable as was represented; and it should be held in mind that, although frequently challenged to produce the name of a single family which could be said to have been unjustly dispossessed, the Roman Catholics never have attempted to substantiate, in any one instance, the charge of cruelty or outrage — a fact which can only be accounted for by the extreme difficulty of finding a single case in which, upon inquiry, it would not be found that the provocations and the offences of the individuals afforded some justification at least for the retaliatory severity with which they were treated.

Many of these families settled in Connaught, where, for some time, they conducted themselves very well. But the old adage, "the wild duck to the bog again," was in their instance strikingly verified; for when the French landed in this country, they, to a man, joined the invaders.[64]

This was, probably, the most critical period of the history of Ireland. The United Irishmen were now completely organized, and waited but the first opportunity to throw off the English yoke, and proclaim the country an independent republic. Their leaders were men of great ability, and with all the zeal and all the courage which their cause demanded. They had become inspired by a passionate persuasion that the liberty and the happiness of their native land were inseparably bound up with their project of dismemberment; and, notwithstanding the disastrous consequences of French fraternization to those unhappy countries which had solicited its embraces, and found oppression where they expected redress, the Irish patriots hesitated not to invite the cooperation of France, for the purpose of enabling them to accomplish the overthrow of British rule, and in the hope that when that was accomplished they would be enabled, of themselves, to maintain their independence — a vain and visionary expectation, which only proves the strong anti-Anglican feeling by which these men were animated, and that, when the passions of a party are once powerfully engaged, the most obvious suggestions of reason and expediency will be disregarded.

Wolfe Tone was a man of spirit and humanity.[65] He possessed the enthusiasm of a poet, and the enterprise and the valour of a soldier. In conversation, there were few men who so gained upon his hearers, by the point and vivacity of his remarks, and the unaffected earnestness and sincerity of his whole demeanour. But in public debate he was by no means equal to many who were far his inferiors in moral and intellectual qualifications. There hung about him a bashfulness which he could not shake off, and which gave him somewhat the appearance of a woman in male attire, making an awkward effort to perform some feat of strength or of activity. Still, his indomitable energy and perseverance gave him a kind of forty-horse power amongst the Irish revolutionists; and he might be truly described as the great political steam-engine, without the aid of which nothing important was to be effected.

France was, at this time, in all the horrors of civil war; and yet it was to France, to blood-stained and revolutionary France, this amiable and gifted man looked for what he called the regeneration of Ireland! Never did I see a greater instance of the baneful effects of infidelity. Wolfe Tone was altogether without any other than what was called natural religion, which bears much the same relation to Christianity that moonlight in a sylvan grotto does to the meridian sun. It was altogether incapable of presenting, to a mind like his, objects by which such a mind might be permanently attracted or profitably occupied; and both his intellect and his affections were far too ardent and too active to remain altogether disengaged. When we do not habitually dwell upon those things by the contemplation of which we may be exalted and purified, the chances are many that we will dwell on those things by which very different results may be produced. And so it was with Wolfe Tone. Politics became his religion; the works of Thomas Payne his Bible;[66] Ireland regenerated into pure republicanism, the object of his heart's idolatry; and almost every measure was sanctified in his eyes as it appeared to him to conduce to this end. Let others blame the criminal and the traitor; I cannot contemplate the untimely fate of this ill-starred man without feelings in which compassion predominates. But alas! When the light that is in us is darkness, how great is that darkness!

Having been permitted, by the generosity of the government, to depart out of the kingdom, under circumstances of suspicious connexion with convicted traitors, for which his life must have paid the forfeit, Wolfe Tone embarked for America, from whence he proceeded to France, in order to lay before the French government a memorial, setting forth the then state of Ireland, with a view to the obtaining of the aid necessary to carry into effect his revolutionary designs. The issue of his disastrous expedition is well known; and I shall only here add respecting it, that never did the hand of God more clearly appear than in that state of the elements which prevented the landing of the French troops, at a time when their arrival in force, and under such a leader as Hoche, might have been so fatal.[67] But I must avail myself of the memorial of Wolfe Tone, addressed to the government of France, in order to show, from the most unexceptionable authority, the state of parties which at that time existed, and the utter and monstrous falsehood of the charges which have been made against the Orangemen of Ireland. The reader will perceive that this was written nearly twelve months after the formation of the first Orange lodge, and that the body was so utterly unknown, as not to be noticed even once in the memorial.

> "In the year 1791, the dissenters of Belfast, which is the principal city in of Ulster, and, as it were, the metropolis of that great party, formed the first club of united Irishmen; so called because in that club, for the first time in Ireland, dissenters and Catholics were seen together in harmony and union. A similar club was immediately formed in Dublin, which became speedily famous for its publications, and the sufferings of its members, many of whom were thrown into prison by the government, whose terror at this rising spirit of union amongst the people may be estimated from the severity with which they persecuted those who were most active in promoting it. This persecution, however, far from quelling the spirit, only served to make the people more cautious and guarded in their measures. Means have been adopted to spread similar clubs throughout Ulster, the seat of the dissenting power, the object of which is to subvert the tyranny of England, to establish the independence of Ireland, and to frame a free republic on the broad basis of liberty and equality. These clubs were rapidly filled, and extended in June last over above two-thirds of that province. I am satisfied that by this time they embrace the whole of it, and comprise the activity and energy of the dissenters of Ireland, including also numbers of the most spirited and intelligent of the Catholic body. The members are all bound by an oath of secrecy, and could, on a proper occasion, I have not the smallest doubt, raise the entire force of the province of Ulster, the most populous, the most warlike, and the most informed quarter of the nation.

"For the Catholics, from what has been said of their situation, it will appear that little previous arrangement would be necessary to insure their unanimous support of any measure which held out to them a chance of bettering their condition; yet they also have an organization, commencing about the same time with the clubs last mentioned, but comprising Catholics only. Until within these few months, this organization baffled the most active vigilance of the Irish government, unsuccessfully employed to discover its principles, and to this hour they are, I believe, unapprised of its extent. The fact is, that in June last it embraced the whole peasantry of the provinces of Ulster, Leinster, and Connaught three-fourths of the nation; and I have little doubt but it has since extended into Munster, the remaining province. These men, who are called Defenders, are completely organized on a military plan, divided according to their respective districts, and officered by men chosen by themselves. The principle of their union is implicit obedience to the orders of those whom they have elected for their generals, and whose object is the emancipation of their country, the subversion of English usurpation, and the bettering the condition of the wretched peasantry of Ireland. The eyes of the whole body, which may be said, almost without a figure, to be the people of Ireland, are turned with the most anxious expectation to France for assistance and support. The oath of their union recites, 'that they will be faithful to the united nations of France and Ireland;' and several of them have already sealed it with their blood. I suppose there is no instance of a conspiracy — if a whole people can be said to conspire — which has continued for so many years as this has done, where the secret has been so religiously kept, and where, in so vast a number, so few traitors have been found.

"The organization of defenders embraces the whole peasantry of Ireland, being Catholics. There is also a further organization of the Catholics, which is called the General Committee, and to which I have already alluded. This was a representative body, chosen by the Catholics at large, and consisting of the principal merchants and traders, the members of professions, and a few of the remaining Catholic gentry of Ireland, This body, which has met repeatedly in the capital, at the same time with the parliament, and has twice within four years sent ambassadors to the King of England,

> possesses a very great influence on the minds of the Catholics throughout the nation, and especially decides the movements of the city of Dublin; a circumstance whose importance, when well directed, it is unnecessary to suggest to men so enlightened as those who compose the government of France. It is true that, by a late act of the Irish legislature, this body is prevented from meeting in a representative capacity; but the individuals who compose it still exist, and this act, without diminishing their power or influence, has still more alienated their minds from the British government in Ireland, against which they were already sufficiently, and with great reason, exasperated. It is but justice to the General Committee, in whose service I had the honour to be during the whole of their activity, and whose confidence I had the good fortune to acquire and retain, to say, that there is nowhere to be found men of purer patriotism, more sincerely attached to the principles of liberty, or who would be more likely, in an arduous crisis, to conduct themselves with ability and firmness. I can add, from my personal knowledge, that a great majority of those able and honest men who compose it are sincere republicans, warmly attached to the cause of France, and, as Irishmen and as Catholics, doubly bound to detest the tyranny and the domination of England, which has so often deluged their country with their best blood."

Such is the statement of Wolfe Tone, of which your readers will, I am persuaded, excuse the insertion, as it is important to have such a witness to such facts as he relates; because, had they rested upon my own unsupported allegations, I might be justly suspected of having coloured them for the purpose of giving plausibility to my own peculiar views. But Wolfe Tone periled his life and fortune upon the truth of the representations set forth in his memorial; and if the Orange institution had not been established, and if it had not acted as the queen bee of sound religious and political principles, associating all classes and descriptions of loyal men for the maintenance of social order, I cannot entertain the slightest doubt that the views of the sagacious enthusiast would have been realized, and Ireland would have been severed from the British empire

I shall reserve, sir, for another opportunity my vindication of the Orange institution from the calumnies by which it has been assailed, and my reasons for believing that its preservation and its extension are as necessary at present as they were at any former time. I shall also, I think, be able to justify the grounds upon which it is, as far as Roman Catholics are concerned, an exclusive association.[68] Meanwhile, I cannot conclude without noticing the instruction which may be derived from the Memoirs of Wolfe Tone. We there have the history of the origin of the late rebellion in Ireland, in a form so authentic, as to silence every doubt, and in a style so lively and graphical, as to engage and interest almost every reader. This able man exhibits treason in all its varieties and degrees, from the first faint conception, until it opened into overt acts, and as it was modified by the dispositions and characters of those to whom it was communicated or by whom it was concocted. The reader may there see the plausible representations by which it was masked, as long as concealment was expedient, and the ferocious energy with which it was manifested when the time had come for throwing off disguise. He may see the process by which the people were stirred up, and the arts by which the government were deluded. The characters, too, who figured at that momentous period are sketched, by one who knew them well, with great spirit and fidelity. The cautious daring of Grattan, the more reckless intrepidity of Archibald Hamilton Rowan, the determined republican energy and the turbulent vanity of James Napper Tandy, the eloquence, the plausibility, and the egotism of John Keogh, are all drawn to the life, and illustrated by various citations from their speeches, their writings, and their conduct.[69] The self-renouncing enthusiasm of Emmet is also well described, and contrasts finely with the wily dexterity which marked the conduct of the present Lord Chancellor of Ireland.[70] In short, I cannot but regard these volumes as a kind of glass bee-hive of sedition, in which men are able to see all the processes by which the industrious insects contained within it are severally elaborating their appointed work, until a political poison was produced by which the life of the monarchy was endangered.

I shall now, sir, for the present, conclude, hoping at an early opportunity to be able to dispose of the remaining topics, the discussion of which may enable us to form a correct judgment of the utility and importance of the Orange institution, as it now exists, and which, I maintain, presents the only effectual antiseptic to the contagion of those pestilent principles, which were never more rife than they are at this moment, and which, if suffered to prevail, must lead to the destruction of the empire.

I remain, Sir, your faithful and obliged

MONTANUS, Co. Down.

SECOND LETTER FROM AN OLD ORANGEMAN

Dublin University Magazine, September, 1835.

TO THE EDITOR OF THE DUBLIN UNIVERSITY MAGAZINE.

SIR, — Your promptitude in attending to my last communication entitles you to at least a similar promptitude on my part in following up the subject of it, and communicating, in plain simple language, such further facts and reasons as occur to me justificatory of the Orange Institution. This I shall do without preface or circumlocution; as I possess neither the time, nor the temper, nor the ability for that amplification and adornment by which the society, of which I would rather be thought the historian than the advocate, may be set off to most advantage; and even if I did, I might perhaps be of opinion that truths, such as I have to state, can gain but little by adventitious aids, and are, when unadorned, adorned the most.

In my last I gave, in the words of Theobald Wolfe Tone, an unexaggerated picture of the state of Ireland contemporaneous with the origin of the Orange Institution. Nothing could be more deplorable. The revolutionary leaven was working itself rapidly through the mass of the people, and the anarchists entertained the confident hope, that, in a very short time, Ireland would be regenerated after the French model, and British connection given to the winds. The reader has seen what good grounds there were for these anticipations, which, I fearlessly assert, that nothing but the counter organization, which commenced upon the field of the Diamond fight, prevented from being, in all respects, realized.

Previously to the year 1795, Ulster was the most disturbed part of Ireland. Since 1796 it has been the most tranquil. Surely this simple and indisputable fact ought to make the most determined enemies of the Orange Institution hesitate in ascribing to it the turbulence and the bloodshed which unhappily disgrace other parts of the country. Such an allegation speaks much for the audacity of assertion which distinguishes one party, but is by no means complimentary to the extent of credulity which is calculated on in the people at large.

I remember that when Mr. O'Connell was under examination before the committee on the state of Ireland in 1825, he was asked how he could reconcile his representations of the conduct of the Orangemen with the peaceable state of that part of the country where they chiefly prevailed. His answer was a denial of the fact. He stated that Ulster was not as peaceful as was represented; and he instanced, in proof of his position, the burning of Wild Goose Lodge, and the rising under Russell at the time of Emmet's insurrection. I believe that no two instances more clearly confirmatory of an opposite hypothesis could be adduced. The affair at Wild Goose Lodge will long be remembered as one of those Romish atrocities which throw all ordinary barbarism into the shade, and vindicate for the professors of the papal creed in this country a pre-eminence in cold-blooded depravity which puts them immeasurably beyond the most inhuman savages.[71] And the attempt which poor Russell made to excite a disloyal feeling in a county which but a few years before had been reticulated, as it were, by a net-work of treason, only proves how rapidly the loyal principle must have revived, and how completely the people were disabused of the republican prejudices, which, on former occasions, rendered them an easy prey to the enemies of the constitution. Let any unprejudiced reader compare the statement which Wolfe Tone gives of the political condition of the north of Ireland in 1796, with the fact, that, in 1803, a man so popular and so accomplished as his friend Russell was not able to rally round him more than thirteen or fourteen drunken and infatuated followers, and he will see evidence of a moral revolution in men's feelings and principles, as striking as any recorded in history.

Then let him inquire the cause of this, and I defy him to trace it to anything but the prevalence of the Orange Institution.[72]

As I have been favoured with a copy of the evidence taken before the special committee at present sitting on the Orange Society, I shall, in the course of this letter, largely avail myself of it. The following is the statement of the Rev. Mortimer O'Sullivan:[73]

> "I saw that the north of Ireland, in which the Orange societies extensively prevailed, was tranquil, and I saw reason to believe that its tranquillity was owing to the Orange Institution. As to the general fact, that the north of Ireland has been tranquil, that life and property are more secure there than in other parts of the country, and outrages far less frequent and revolting, it need not rest on the testimony of any interested individual. Any honourable member who will do the Irish Protestants the justice to enquire into their case can satisfy himself. He can ascertain what is the amount of military force required in the north, what is the strength of police; he can ascertain the state of the calendar of crime, of coroners' inquests, of judges' charges; and if it be apparent that Ulster is almost wholly free from outrages, and that there has been a species of tacit recognition of the tranquil and peaceable state of that province, in the small military and police force stationed in it; a recognition conceded not only by those governments which might be considered favourable to Protestants, but by Whig governments as well as Tory, the tranquillity of Ulster cannot any longer be disputed. That such testimonies have been offered in its favour, it is in the power of any honorable member to satisfy himself. I not only saw the country tranquil, but had reason to believe that its peacefulness was mainly owing to the conduct and the combination of the Orange societies. I found that, from the year 1760, when, after the landing of Thurot the first disturbances commenced in Ireland, up to the year 1798, Ulster was much disturbed and disaffected.[74] Its character was at that time such as may be known from contained, I think, in a paper found on a passage in one of Wolfe Tone's papers, Jackson, who was appointed as delegate to France.[75] The force necessary may be not more than 20,000, nor less than 10,000 men. Suppose them 10,000, 7000 should land in the west, and having secured and fortified a landing

> place, should advance into the middle of the country. At the same time 3000 should land immediately at the capital, and seize on all the stores, and such persons as might be troublesome. In that event, the north would rise to a man! Such was the character of Ulster in 1794. Towards the close of the following year the Orange society was formed. The rebellion took place in 1798; and in 1803, when Russell, a man of very popular manners and strong claims on the good will of the people, went down to try whether he could excite insurrection in the north, to second Emmet's attempt in Dublin, his utmost efforts were not able to procure more than fourteen followers. When the Orange Institution became organized, the character of the north altered, and, from that time to the present, 34 years from the date of the Union with England, notwithstanding the various tumults and disturbances which have taken place in Ireland, there never has been an application of the insurrection act to the north, nor a necessity for it. I looked, therefore, upon the tranquillity of the north, and the power of the Orange Society as not merely co-existing, but as connected, to a great degree, in the relation of cause and effect; and, having found in the society, after the strictest inquiry, no ground of offence either from the disposition of the members, or the character of the system, I looked upon it that the critical circumstances of the times demanded of me the joining myself with the body."

Such is the statement of the mildest and most gentle-hearted of divines, whose retiring habits, and aversion to the obstreperous din of politics are well known to his personal friends, and whom nothing short of the imperious conviction, that the best interests of religion would be hazarded by his neutrality, could have drawn from the sweet privacy of his pastoral retirement. His evidence is most instructive, and ought to be published, in a cheap and compendious tract, for the information of the public at large. I shall not at present say more of it than that it fully sustains his very high reputation, and must do much to disabuse those who read it of many of their prejudices against the Orange Institution. Were the true state of the country only fully known, the society, which furnishes the only bulwark against popery and radicalism, would not long want for able and intrepid defenders.

It will, I believe, now be admitted, on the part of every candid inquirer, that the Orange Institution was justified in its origin, and served most important purposes when a rebellious spirit pervaded the land; but, this being granted, it may be assumed, that it was, itself, the cause of many evils, by provoking angry collisions between classes of persons differing in their religious and political views, who might, if it were not for the July processions, have lived together in very tolerable peace and harmony.[76] Now, I am old enough to remember the state of Ulster before the year 1795, and I fearlessly assert that the angry collisions of adverse parties were much more frequent and much more envenomed than they have been since. In fact, before the Orange Institution arose, there were three periods of the year during which the Protestant party used to celebrate remarkable epochs in the life of their great deliverer William the Third; so that the only effect which the Orange system had in that respect was, to discontinue two of these political festivals. Instead, therefore, of making that system bear the blame of increasing, it is entitled to credit for diminishing party violence, which is vastly less now than it was previous to the existence of Orange organization, and which, I may say, were it not for the growing intolerance and the growing insolence of the popish faction, would not, at present, have any existence.

I well remember when Roman Catholics joined in procession round the statue of King William, on the 12th of July, and were as ardent as any Protestants in their demonstration of loyal enthusiasm on those annual celebrations of the triumph of civil and religious liberty. They were, then, unemancipated; and I must say that their demeanour on these occasions was what first impressed me and others with the policy of striking off those restrictions by which they were aggrieved and putting them, in all respects, upon a level with their Protestant fellow subjects.[77] But, strange to say, precisely in proportion as the penal code was mitigated, did they become intolerant of those anniversaries by which the victory of the Boyne was commemorated, until, when every vestige of the disabling statutes was removed, these anniversaries were felt to be altogether intolerable. How is this to be accounted for? How can it be accounted for by any Protestants, without supposing that popish views and popish prejudices still survive, and that every acquisition of power or of influence which they have made, is only valued by them as it may serve to facilitate the accomplishment of ulterior objects?

That collisions have taken place, and that conflicts have ensued at these processions in latter times, I very well know. But I know, also, that they always occurred in consequence of aggressions on the part of Roman Catholics. This has been demonstrated in many instances, in which the parties were brought before courts of justice, where it invariably appeared that had the Protestant party been suffered to proceed in peace with their annual celebration, they would have injured no man. Now, had the Roman Catholics been interrupted in a similar manner, during their procession and festivities on the 17th of March, I, at least, would not offer a single word in excuse for the Protestants by whom they might be thus molested.[78] And how does the case differ when the aggressions proceed from the other side; and how can the Protestants be expected to feel when the aggressors are countenanced by the government, and their illegal proceedings made the ground of an act forbidding processions in which they and their ancestors rejoiced from the period when the victory of the Boyne gave security to the British constitution in Ireland?[79]

This is a case in which I know that wise and good men differ from me. Lord Stanley differs from me.[80] Sir Robert Peel differs from me.[81] But I do think that this is not the only instance in which expediency has been made to stand in the place of principle on the part of both these able men; and I am too old fashioned to understand even the expediency of creating a new crime in order to avoid punishing an old one. Nothing was clearer than that the Protestants, in assembling to commemorate the 12th of July, violated no law. Nothing was clearer than that the Roman Catholics, in violently opposing them on such occasions, violated many laws. And the course pursued by our legislators has been to make a new law, denouncing processions, in order to avoid carrying into effect an old law, by which the parties creating a disturbance at such processions might be visited with the punishment which their misconduct would deserve. Surely it is not wonderful that the Protestants should feel themselves aggrieved by a proceeding such as this, and that an unusual stimulus should have been given to the insolence of their opponents. And I fairly confess that when I consider the temper in which that enactment was passed, and the parties against whom it was directed, I see infinitely more cause to admire the degree in which it has been complied with, than to be surprised that there have been a few instances in which its provisions have been disregarded. But as it is now on all hands agreed that processions are to be given up, this is a part of the subject which I will be excused for not pursuing any farther.

It is objected that the Orange is an exclusive association. It is, as far as Roman Catholics are concerned. No papist can be a member of it. One of the objects which it proposes is the preservation of the Protestant religion. And how could the obligation to be assisting in the promotion of such an object, be cordially or sincerely undertaken by members of the church of Rome? It is also to be considered, that it was a Roman Catholic confederacy which gave rise to the Orange Institution; a confederacy having for its object Protestant extirpation; and nothing could have been either more natural or more reasonable than that exceptions should have been taken against the professors of a creed, which seemed, at least, to countenance the most revolting principles, and to give a kind of religious sanction to the most abominable crimes?

It was believed by Protestants that Roman Catholics would not keep faith with heretics.[82] It was believed that the tenets of their church were intolerant and persecuting, and that they only wanted opportunity in order to carry them fully into effect. This persuasion, no doubt, had its influence on those by whom the original regulations of the Orange Institution were drawn up, and, if well founded, entirely justifies their exclusion of a body of men who never could sympathise with the feelings of Orangemen, and who could only give the evidence of their treachery to one system as a proof of their fidelity to the other.

But, it was not merely upon theological grounds that Roman Catholics were excluded. Their conduct served to discriminate them from Protestants in a way that clearly showed there could be, between the two bodies neither unity of sentiment nor cordiality of cooperation. I need not here load your pages by an enumeration of the atrocities which gave a peculiar character to the former, as it is sufficient merely to allude to the dreadful affairs at Fork Hill, the massacre on Wexford bridge, the burnings at Scullabogue, at Wildgoose Lodge, at the house of the Sheas in Tipperary, and in various other places, to show that the Roman Catholics were distinguished from the Protestants not less by feeling than by principle, and that while the former were under the influence of the baleful bigotry by which they were actuated, the latter never could be expected to associate with them for constitutional objects.[83]

It was, in point of fact, the manifestation of this dreadful spirit that led to the separation between Roman Catholics and Protestants, to which, in a great measure the defeat of the rebellion of 1798 is to be attributed. And if those who were united as rebels, in the cause of treason, could not continue combined, because of the antipathies of Roman Catholics to Protestants as heretics, it is not to be wondered at, that loyal men should have been disinclined to admit them into an association which was only rendered necessary by their known antipathy to the established church, and their scarcely suppressed desire to overthrow British authority in Ireland.

And this leads me naturally to the circumstance which first caused the great spread of Orangeism in the north of Ireland.

It was in Wexford that the spirit of popery most decidedly manifested itself, when in 1798 some little success attended the first outbreak of the rebellion in Ireland; cruelties the most inhuman and remorseless, were perpetrated upon such Protestants as fell into their power, insomuch that many, whose political bias was entirely against the government, and who desired a severance of British connection, felt that they were but blindly instrumental in erecting a spiritual tyranny, to which, sooner or later, they themselves must fall victims. Affidavits verifying the facts of some of these atrocities, were procured by the late Sir Hardinge Giffard, and their extensive circulation through the north of Ireland, where they were eagerly read, caused such a reaction in favour of loyalty, and so lively a horror of popish perfidy and cruelty, that the disaffected were, in that part of the country, speedily shorn of all their power, and a strong hold of sound conservative principles erected, as it were, upon the ruins of a den of treasons.[84] The natural manner in which this feeling manifested itself, was by a large accession to the Orange Association; men of rank and property encouraged their tenants and retainers to connect themselves with that body, as the most satisfactory mode of manifesting their attachment to church and state, and the most unequivocal demonstration of their antipathy to Irish traitors. And thus it was that that change was produced in Ulster, which converted it from the focus of sedition which Wolf Tone describes it, in his memorial to the French Directory in 1796, into the peaceable and loyal province which his friend Russell found it in 1803, when he made his insane attempt to rouse the people on the occasion of Emmet's insurrection.

There is nothing which provokes the sneers of liberals more than allusions to those persecuting dogmas of the church of Rome which are to be found in the works of her accredited theologians. These dogmas, they maintain, belong rather to the age when they were invented, than to the churches in which they were received; and any notion that they can be practically revived at the present day, is an absurdity that carries with it its own refutation. It was in allusion to such a notion that Lord Plunket made use of the well-known phrase, that those who adopted it, and grounded their adoption of it upon statements and documents to be found in the works of divines, and in the decrees of councils, treated history as if it were nothing better than an old almanack.[85] Now it has always appeared to me, that, in this particular, our would-be philosophers overshoot the mark, and make far too little account of the insensible influence of such a system as popery over the great mass of its votaries. In that system it is perfectly clear, that the dogmas above alluded to, were once received, and it is, I believe, equally clear that they never have been rejected. We know the deep veneration with which Roman Catholics are taught and expected to regard the church; and that their religion chiefly consists in giving an unreasoning and unhesitating obedience to its dictates. They, in fact, only know the gospel through the church whereas, Protestants only know the church through the gospel; a difference too, which must give rise to a corresponding distinction between the classes thus opposed, and cause the former to regard all who desert from their notion of a living infallible authority upon earth, in precisely the same light as the latter regard those who reject revealed religion. Protestants are, in fact, considered in the light of infidels, who have rejected the true faith, but who cannot, by their rejection of it, divest themselves of their baptismal obligations, but still continue, although rebels against the authority, subject to the dominion of the church of Rome, and at any time liable to be reduced to their allegiance. It may be that many of them have never directly traced the inferences from the principles which they maintained — it may be that in many of them the spirit of the age has so far mitigated their principles that no such inference would appear to be fairly deducible from them, or, if shown to be fairly deduced, the principles would be renounced rather than the inferences adopted. All this may be, and much of this, no doubt, is true. It is in fact, from the latter class that the most enlightened converts from popery have recently been made; and it is by such an exposure of the principles of the church of Rome, as may seem to impress upon the minds of that class the real character of the creed which they have adopted, more from accident than conviction, that we must rest our best hopes of the moral regeneration of Ireland. But, allowing everything which can be claimed for superior enlightenment at the present day, and allowing also that the spirit of the age is adverse to the unmitigated intolerance of former times, it will still make a very great difference to the gross bulk of Irish Romanists, whether the genius of their religion be essentially of a tolerant or a persecuting nature. It may be that, in times of ordinary tranquillity, when no considerable religious excitement prevails, that the worst tenets of popery may be entertained without any offensive external manifestation; they may, in fact, be rather latent than revealed. Where and when protestantism is latitudinarian and indolent, popery may be sluggish and dormant. But, let different circumstances present themselves, let excitement prevail, let the professors of one creed exhibit an ardour and an interest in the diffusion of what they believe to be the truth, which may provoke a corresponding and antagonist zeal in those to whom they are opposed, and then it will be seen what the principles are by which the latter are in reality actuated; then, it may be, that for the first time, they will become conscious of the influence of these principles themselves.

When I hear Roman Catholics disclaim the persecuting tenets of their church, although I distrust, I do not disbelieve them.

On the contrary, I entertain no doubt that they are, at the time, perfectly sincere in their asseverations. When the prophet told the Jewish king that he would, at a future time, commit some great iniquity, the latter indignantly exclaimed, "Is thy servant a dog that he should do this thing?" But he did it.[86] Did it, although both the letter and the spirit of his religion were against it; did it, although it was prophetically denounced to him, as he could not but be deeply persuaded that he was thus transgressing the commandments of Almighty God? How much more prone would he have been to the perpetration of it, if he could be persuaded that he was thereby doing God a service — if the spirit of his religion discountenanced it not? but, on the contrary, by various decrees, and precepts and examples, (which, as long as he unhesitatingly received his creed, he could not deny to have great weight, if not paramount authority,) encouraged every project for the humbling of heretics and the exaltation of the church, no matter how opposed to justice and humanity? Now, this is precisely the case of the Roman Catholics of Ireland. The late exposure of Dens's Theology shows that such are the precepts of their religion;[87] and on every one occasion where their prejudices were inflamed and their passions excited, their conduct has been uniformly conformable thereto. They have shown that neither promises nor oaths could restrain them, when by disregarding promises and oaths the destruction of an heretical church might be accomplished. They have shown that neither gratitude nor honesty could influence them, when by withholding the Protestant pastors' lawful dues, and menacing their lives, a prospect was afforded of their extermination.[88]

I will not stop to instance the crime and the outrages by which this position might be illustrated; suffice it to say, they are most bloody and most atrocious. But, however revolting to humanity, and even contrary to nature, there is not one of them that may not be traced to the dogmas or the influences of the Roman Catholic religion. This may not be seen or felt in times of quiet, when the government is strong, but it will become deplorably manifest whenever the state of the country is such as to encourage turbulence and disorder. There is not an individual engaged in resistance to tithe, who believes that such resistance amounts to robbery, and there is not an assassin whose hands have been embrued in the blood of a Protestant clergyman, who can persuade himself that he thus incurs the guilt of murder. Every evil passion of which their nature is susceptible, is marshalled, as it were, under the sanction of religion. In their most diabolical atrocities they feel as if they were engaged in carrying into effect a sentence pronounced by their church against heretical pravity, and that, instead of adding to their other offences, their conduct in that particular will operate like charity, and serve to cover a multitude of crimes.[89] Such is the state of feeling now universally prevailing amongst the lower classes of the Roman Catholics of Ireland. They are not like Protestants, who live in the light of the Holy Scriptures, and who possess this security, at least against errors in practice, that the precepts and the conduct of their teachers will all be brought to the test of the unerring word of God. No such thing; they only see this word as it pleases its misinterpreters to exhibit it to them;[90] it is converted into a species of lying oracle, only to be consulted when the ends of falsehood are to be attained. The very same kind of jugglery which is practised at Naples upon the blood of St. Januarius, is had recourse to for the purpose of making Holy Scripture bear testimony against itself;[91] texts are parodied and misinterpreted in a manner that makes them give the lie to the context; and even when the truth is exhibited, it falls off upon the eyes of Roman Catholics like light through a discoloured medium, imparting to all surrounding objects the hue of the substance through which it is seen. In short, to them the end of their religion would seem to be the exaltation of their church, while to Protestants the end of the church is the exaltation of religion.

No man can deny the dreadful system of crime at present in operation in this country; no man can deny that both life and property are fearfully insecure.[92] Now, there are very few who have contemplated the characters of our peasantry without perceiving in them much to commend — much to win upon their love and admiration. They are proverbially a kind-hearted and affectionate people, with as little of gall or of bitterness in their composition as is to be found in any peasantry upon the face of the earth. How, then, are we to account for the strong contrast to all this which is exhibited in their conduct? how are we to account for the fact, that not only are they given to the perpetration of enormous crime, but that these crimes are perpetrated with a remorseless barbarity by which the North American savages are outdone, and which could only be paralleled by the familiars of the Inquisition? Manifestly only by supposing that they are under the influence of a creed by which the natural conscience is seared as with a red-hot iron, and which imposes upon them the persuasion that oaths are perjuries where their observance would be prejudicial to the church, and that humanity is weakness when it would interpose any obstacles to the extirpation of those who are believed to be the enemies of true religion. This is the only mode of accounting for the present perverted state both of feeling and principle in Ireland. The nature of the people has been changed by their creed; it has been transmuted from good into evil — indeed it might be said of many of them, that "evil has become their good,"[93] as there is scarcely any extreme of wickedness which is not considered allowable against the persons and properties of an heretical clergy.

All this being so, is it surprising that Roman Catholics should be excluded from the Orange Association?[94] Indeed the only thing to be wondered at is, that they should have complained of such exclusion. They might as well complain of being excluded, while they continue Roman Catholics, from the rites and the privileges of the established church. To do them justice, I never heard them complain of such exclusion until Mr. Sheil and others of their body made it a specific ground of objection to the Orange body, in the investigation which has been just concluded by a special committee of the House of Commons.[95]

No; it was quite impossible for two bodies so directly opposed in feeling and principle, to have amalgamated for any good purpose. In the case of the Irish rebellion the Protestants and Roman Catholics found it impossible to continue united even for a bad one. The Orange institution was established as a rallying-post for the loyalty of Ireland, and it was quite impossible for its founders to overlook the notorious disloyalty of a class of men who were under influences that must, as long as they continued, have rendered their allegiance precarious. They were excluded, because their exclusion was the only means of preserving the integrity of a confederation rendered necessary by the threatening attitude which they assumed, and without which British connexion must have been endangered. But was not this exclusion calculated to give offence? Was it not calculated to provoke an opposite combination? If it did provoke some combination of Roman Catholics, who took some other mode of displaying their loyalty, this, I apprehend, would not be an evil; the two bodies might exist like rivals of the same mistress, and each endeavour to outdo the other in demonstrations of zeal and attachment and this is the only manner in which the Orange Institution would operate, supposing the Roman Catholic to be as loyal as the Protestant community. Upon the contrary, supposing a different result might take place, and the loyal might, by possibility, give rise to a disloyal confederacy; but in this case it would only quicken, and bring into premature development, the disloyalty that would otherwise be latent. In the first case it is almost certain that the two bodies would ultimately coalesce; in the second, the more widely they were discriminated, the better for the peace and the security of the empire.

In point of fact, it was the disloyal that gave rise to the loyal association. Defenderism at first provoked the Orangemen to combine, and Ribbonism now causes them to continue their combination. It is a matter of perfect certainty, confirmed by the evidence of almost every individual who appeared before the Orange committee, either for that body or against them, that an extensive confederacy exists, comprising, probably, three-fourths of the Roman Catholic peasantry, and having for one of its objects the extirpation of the Protestant religion and Protestant name in Ireland. Mr. O'Connell, when questioned respecting this body before the parliamentary committee in 1825, stated his belief that they were a continuation of the old Defender association; and there is much reason to think that he was right.[96] Everything that even he says, is not to be rejected. They seem identified in spirit and in principle with that body, and do not sink a single point below them in hatred of the established church and antipathy to British connexion. The year 1796, the reader has seen, from the Memoirs of Wolf Tone, that this body extended over three provinces in Ireland, and was progressing rapidly over the fourth. How far the Riband system extends has not yet been clearly ascertained; but it is perfectly certain that it is most powerful, that it has proved in many cases too strong for the laws, and that there is no security for life or property without some such protective confederacy as is afforded in the Orange Institution.

As it is not impossible that the nature of this confederacy may yet attract the notice of parliament, I will not compromise the individuals from whom I have had information respecting it by any untimely disclosures. They are bound together by an oath, pledging them to the most ruthless hatred of Protestants, and binding them to be ready at any time to swear falsely in a court of justice, when by so doing the interests of the party may be served. How far the Roman Catholic clergy are identified with or opposed to this body I know not. It is certain that the Ribbonmen look upon them as their friends, and in most instances regard any admonitory language which may be made use of by them when any great atrocities have been perpetrated as language much more of caution than of reproof, and as not intended seriously to militate against their combination. It is a common thing for a defenceless Protestant, in those districts where the Orange system is not strong, to be waylaid and seriously injured, and then to be prosecuted in a court of justice, as though he were the person guilty of the assault, and by the force of perjured testimony to be convicted. I am credibly informed that there are individuals this moment suffering the punishment of imprisonment, only because they were so unfortunate as to have been the victims of aggression such as I have described. Now, in this state of things, in which the law, in reality, is powerless, is it possible that the Protestants can exist in security without some combination by which they may be protected? It is, manifestly, impossible. When the power of their enemies is too great for the laws, by the isolated efforts of individuals it never could be resisted, and any measures which would have the effect of severing the bonds of brotherhood by which Orangemen are united to each other for mutual defence and for the preservation of the public peace, would be but the speedy precursors of Protestant extermination.

Does it not seem most extraordinary that the part of Ireland concerning which an inquiry is instituted is that part of the country which alone is tranquil;[97] and that this is done, if not for the purpose, at least with the certainty of directing the attention of the people of England from that part of the country which alone is disturbed. I may not even conjecture what the designs of the Roman Catholic members were in moving for the committee on Orange societies; but they could not have taken a more effectual means of screening the delinquencies of their own partisans, and securing to them a legislative impunity in their transgressions. While murder and rapine and conflagration are proceeding unchecked in one part of the country,[98] the whole attention of government is absorbed in a minute and vindictive criticism of the conduct of men who are, in another part of the country, the strenuous upholders of the law, and the best friends of British connexion. I remember the story of a gentleman who came post haste for a physician to see a man who was represented as being in extreme danger. The physician lost no time in obeying the summons; and, upon reaching the house, was shown into what was called the sick room, but where, to his surprise, he could see no patient. Upon asking his conductor where the sick man lay, "Oh," says he, "you are yourself the sick man! Do you not know that you are very bad? Come, I must prescribe for you!" It is not necessary to proceed with the narrative, or to show how the worthy doctor was ultimately rescued from his insane guide; but, surely, the case of the Orangemen is not very dissimilar, and I only fear that there is too much method in the madness of those by whom they are to be destroyed to afford them any similar chance of escaping from their nauseous and injurious prescriptions.

Much has been said of the evils likely to arise from having Orange lodges in the army.[99] It is strange that there was no one to observe that they have existed in the army a long time, and that no evil has arisen from them. The demagogue declaimed, with great vehemence, upon the abstract possibility that they might interfere with discipline.[100] But one well authenticated fact that they had so interfered would have told more against the institution than all their declamation, and that one authenticated fact could not be found. On the contrary, the Orange Institution has always been found aiding discipline; and if the system were to be judged of by its merits, it is impossible that it should not be commended. Still, I would say, that as the army is the very place where it is least needed, as exceptions have been taken to marching warrants, no more should be issued,[101] even though the objections against them may proceed from individuals who were members of the assassination committee in 1798, and who would willingly be members of any similar committee at the present day, if it only afforded a reasonable chance of the overthrow of British influence in Ireland.[102]

I may here mention the origin of the Orange system in the army. The taint of Defenderism had infected the troops at the time when the association was first formed, and it was necessary to introduce the antagonist principle in order to its expulsion. It was also suspected that in many instances the officers were not as deeply imbued as they ought to be with constitutional principles, and the men sometimes complained that they could not confide in the fidelity of those who fought at their side, nor rely upon the loyalty of those by whom they were commanded. To remove, therefore, all suspicion, officers and men, in many instances, became Orangemen; and the consequence was, an increased efficiency, of which no one had any reason to complain but their enemies. Treason was defeated, rebellion was put down, and British influence was preserved in Ireland. Is it, therefore, to be wondered at that the Orange Institution should be peculiarly disrelished by the advocates for a repeal of the Union?

It is painful to think that the only individuals, not of their body, who seem to know the value of the Orange Institution, as a means of preserving the integrity of the empire, are their bitterest enemies. O'Connell has painfully felt the counteracting influence which it has exerted against his anti-Anglican designs; and Mr. Sheil well knows that in its organization is to be found an efficiency by which the most desperate projects of the popish party must be defeated. Therefore, they are moving heaven and earth for its destruction. Therefore, no expedient is declined, by those gentlemen and their followers, by which its character may be blackened and its utility disparaged. All this is natural. Those gentlemen are playing their own game: they act under the full persuasion that, by striking a fatal blow at the existence of the

Orange system, almost every obstacle will be removed which could impede them in the attainment of their most daring revolutionary objects. Strange that the friends of our institution cannot or will not take a hint from their enemies! They may depend upon it that the Irish papists know what they are about. They are wise in their generation: but their wisdom would, in this particular, be of little avail, if it were not seconded by our infatuation. The fact I believe to be, that Lord Stanley's prejudices against the Orange system are not to be overcome, and the leaders of the Conservative party seem willing to sacrifice its interests for his cooperation.

The following extract from the examination of the Rev. M. O'Sullivan, before the select committee, is very important:[103]

> "Q. Now, there being six millions and a half of Roman Catholics in Ireland, thus armed with the powers you have adverted to, although your arguments might have been strong against Roman Catholic emancipation, yet, now that it has been passed, and that its effects have been enhanced by reform, and must be enhanced by ulterior measures of a similar nature, how is it possible to maintain that system of which you conceive the Orange society is the prop?
>
> "A. I think the Orange societies may be the human means of preventing the massacre which will otherwise attend the separation of Ireland from England. The question has referred to the great increase of power conferred upon the Roman Catholics; and it is well known that in every instance in which the Roman Catholics have obtained an increase of power it has been followed by the announcement of new demands. It would be absurd to suppose that in the existing state of things, the great mass of the Roman Catholic people in Ireland can contentedly acquiesce in their present condition. The gentry are put into the possession of place and power, and have more than the due proportion of power which property would naturally confer; but the great mass of the Roman Catholic people remain exactly as they were in past years, in circumstances of extreme distress — perhaps as wretched a peasantry, as far as condition causes wretchedness, as can be

found. There is, therefore, in their circumstances, much to keep discontent alive; and discontent, when power is connected with it, will naturally encourage daring projects and expectations. I look upon it, therefore, that the minds of the Roman Catholic people of Ireland will be set upon effecting the objects which they have in view, of reclaiming lands from Protestant possessors; and they will look to effecting a repeal of the Union; and I honestly state my feeling of the importance of the Orange society, that, when matters have come to the last issue, however dreadful the alternative, it is better that there should be a battle than a massacre. The Orange society, if it exist in force, will perhaps moderate the fury of an excited people; they may make a display of strength which will prevent a massacre, or even a battle. If the society be broken up, I can see no sure resource for the Protestants of Ireland. I can affirm, with the most perfect sincerity, that these are the impressions on my mind; and it was under these impressions that I joined the Orange society.

"Q. Can you conceive that, in the course of time, the Roman Catholic church in Ireland may become as mitigated as in other countries?

"A. No; because national discontent inflames it. Indeed, looking to the spirit of that church, as set forth in the theology of Dens, and seeing a republication of such a book as his recommended by the Roman Catholic bishops in Ireland, and constituting a species of professional library for the priesthood, I should feel a mitigation of their intolerance to be almost hopeless.

"Q.—But you are aware that, theoretically, the same doctrine is allowed in the Netherlands, and yet it does not influence the people?

"A. Not as yet.

"Q. In case, after the disclosures which have been made of the extensive organization of the Orange body in this committee, this body should be permitted to exist, do you not think it extremely probable that the Roman Catholics will, upon the other hand, enter into an organization, not composed of the mere rabble, which constituted the principal ingredients in the riband association, and societies of a similar character, but composed of the Roman Catholic gentry of the country, men of education and intelligence, and advancing in intellectual professions, every day acquiring property, and who, you must feel, are already armed with very extensive power, both inside the House of Commons and without?

"A. Nothing more desirable for the Protestants of Ireland can be imagined than that they should do so, if they introduced such principles as influence the Orangemen into the confederation. The effect would be, to break up that dreadful conspiracy in which the great mass of the Irish Roman Catholics are now leagued together.

"Q. Do you not conceive that such an organization as has been mentioned, composed exclusively of Roman Catholics, an organization which should make its way into the army, and establish lodges in several regiments of the line, would be a most pernicious institution?

"A. I would say, in reply, that if there existed in the country a Protestant organization, and that it was hostile to all members of the church of Rome; and that there was supposed to be a bond, of which there could be exhibited such evidence as the Protestants can show of the obligation which exists amongst the members of the riband societies, in Ireland, and the treasonable societies of which they are a continuance, binding the members to contemplate, and, when practicable, attempt, the extirpation of Roman Catholics; and if there could be produced books belonging to the church of England, having the authority of that church, and constituting the instruction of its priesthood, and that from those books it could be ascertained that Protestants were required to acknowledge the maintaining as a principle that it was right to put Roman Catholics to death for their religious opinions; and if they endeavoured to make proselytes to those opinions, and to extend the conspiracy amongst their fellow subjects, both military and civil — so far would I be from discountenancing such associations

> as those described by the honourable member, that, if the law did not put down, or was not able to put down, the prior confederacy, I would say that Roman Catholics were not only justified but bound to do everything that the law would enable them to do for their mutual protection."

I do trust that the masterly evidence of this able man will be read with the attention which it deserves. It was my intention to explain fully my views respecting the continuance of the Orange Institution, and the important services which it is calculated to answer in a crisis like the present. But I feel that I have already encroached unreasonably on your pages this month, and that the subject may be fittingly resumed when the whole of the evidence which has been taken respecting it is in the hands of the public. Till then, adieu.

MONTANUS, Co. Down.

THIRD LETTER FROM AN OLD ORANGEMAN

Dublin University Magazine, October, 1835.

TO THE EDITOR OF THE DUBLIN UNIVERSITY MAGAZINE.

SIR,

Lord Gosford, in his evidence before the Orange committee, admitted that the principles of the Orange institution are unexceptionably good. He stated also, that the men who compose the body are subjects of whom any sovereign might be proud. But the men and the principles both together formed a 'tertium quid,' so dangerous and so unmanageable, as to excite his strongest reprobation.[104] His lordship did not condescend to give any explanation of this singular phenomenon, or attempt to show how it happened that good men, and good principles, when united, produce bad subjects.[105] Yet such was the proposition which, from his own admission, he was called upon to maintain. He was not, however, very strictly examined as to the connection between his premises and his conclusion; and he had the satisfaction of feeling that he was before a tribunal, who, if on other occasions they could 'strain at a gnat,' in this instance were willing to 'swallow a camel.'

In my last I stated that, long before the institution of the Orange system, the Protestant party were in the habit of celebrating anniversaries, at which Roman Catholics took offence; so that that system is not chargeable with originating such exhibitions; and also, that the number of them was diminished, and not increased, when Orange lodges became established, so that neither is it chargeable with augmenting that source of public mischief. But this point is so important, that I have judged it right to rest it upon something better than my own assertion, and the reader will find my statement fully borne out in the following extract from Barrington's *Historical Memoirs of Ireland*. He thus writes:

> "In 1779 the harsh operation of the penal statutes was aggravated by the triumphs of Protestant supremacy, which were then celebrated throughout Ireland with all the zeal of bacchanalian orgies. A system of political idolatry seemed to have infatuated the whole of the Protestant population, and their devotion to even the statue and the memory of the dead King William the Third, appeared as powerfully efficacious as their loyal attachment to the living monarch, in kindling the fervour of their enthusiasm. Thrice every year the Irish Protestants celebrated the birth and the victories of the Prince of Orange, in a manner peculiarly calculated to revive the animosities of their Catholic fellow-subjects."[106]

I cite this statement for one purpose alone, namely, the clear attestation which the writer bears to the existence of party processions long before the birth of the Orange institution. That they were intended to give offence, or even made a cause of offence, is not so clear, because it is indisputable that Roman Catholics themselves very often joined in them, and continued to do so, according to Mr. O'Connell's statement, when examined on his oath before the House of Lords, until the most objectionable of the penal laws was repealed.[107] And that the one anniversary which the Orange body resolved to keep, was not adopted with any feeling such as the writer of the above extract ascribes to Protestants of a former day, is evident from the fact, that he himself became a member. Yes, reader, Sir Jonah Barrington's name appears upon the books as amongst those of some of the earliest Orangemen in Ireland!

It has, I trust, appeared from my former letters, that the Orange was, in its origin, a strictly defensive institution; and that, in its effects, it amply justified the views of its founders. Revival of loyalty attested its presence, and an increase of security and tranquillity attended its progress. The secret machinations of traitors were defeated, and the open violence of defenderism was restrained. As soon as Protestants began to feel some sense of security, from the character and the extent of the new combinations, it immediately appeared that the cause of the revolutionists had long derived a seeming support from numbers by whom it was secretly detested; for, when it was found that the Orangemen were able to protect themselves, and that, wherever they were established in force, the aggressive violence of the other party was suspended; no sooner did this appear than there was a manifestation of loyalty, which, but a short time before, could have been little suspected; and very many who had been drawn on, by the anarchists, step by step, until they had reached the very verge of the precipice of treason, recoiled from their perilous position with a degree of horror which never left them until they felt themselves securely lodged in the bosom of that constitutional party, upon the growth and the prevalence of which depended the tranquillity of Ireland, and the integrity of the empire.

Yes, when England was menaced by foreign war — when she was assailed by domestic treason — when Ireland was convulsed by civil war, and her coasts hourly threatened with invasion, the Orangemen were found a help in time of need, by whose aid, under Providence, the national salvation was accomplished. Had the institution not arisen, it is my firm belief that the country would have been undone. Her loyal men, scattered and dispirited, could have made no effectual stand against the disciplined and enthusiastic revolutionists to whom they were opposed, and by whom they would have been crushed, one by one, until no one was left who might dare to stand up for the constitution. But, by acting together with concert and energy, they soon were felt to be formidable. Every day saw an accession to their numbers. The gentry and nobility of the country, Whig as well as Tory, were desirous of being enrolled amongst their body; and some of the names upon the list of their early members, were those of individuals whose whole political lives had been previously devoted to projects which had won for them much of popular regard, and which had for their object Irish independence. Lord

Northland and Mr. Brownlow encouraged the growth of Orange principles amongst their tenants and dependents;[108] Plowden, the popish historian, and the inveterate and persevering enemy of the Protestant name, abuses the Marquis of Hertford, the Marquis of Abercorn, the Earl of Londonderry, Mr. Cope, Mr. Richardson, and others, for their patronage of the institution, which, with a kind of suicidal indiscretion, he stigmatizes as sanctioning an oath of extermination; as if it were possible that such noblemen and gentlemen could, for one moment, countenance it, if it were indeed the nefarious and abominable thing that it was represented.[109]

The reader has seen how rapidly Ulster became tranquillized. It was in the time of Wolfe Tone the hot-bed of sedition. It became the very citadel of loyalty, as was found by his unhappy friend Russell, when he made his desperate experiment upon it in 1803. I defy the wit of man to give any other explanation of this great change than is to be found in the prevalence of the Orange association. It furnishes one of the sublimest proofs on record, that a few men, united for a righteous and holy purpose, are able to countervail a multitude of enemies; for still the Orangemen were few in number, when compared with those to whom they were opposed. But their hearts were sound, and their cause was good, and they were not at that time regarded with a vindictive jealousy by the government of the country.

There is one other instance in which, as I conceive, the Conservative effects of the institution very clearly appeared, and which I cannot do better than give in the words of one from whom I have before quoted. He thus expressed himself at the Conservative Society, on the 9th of September, 1834;[110]

> "The mission of Mr. Lawless to the North, and the temper in which it was undertaken, are well remembered;[111] when, with a mass of followers consisting of one hundred and forty-four thousand men, he advanced to enter the 'Black North,' as Mr. Wyse, the historian, as well as a distinguished member of the

Catholic Association, informs us.[112] From Mr. Wyse, also, we have an account of the numbers which assembled, and the spirit which animated these tumultuary gatherings, in his acknowledgment, that many felt a great repugnance to this summons, (to attend what were called reconciliation meetings,)[113] but the secret combination law of the county of Tipperary was so well known, and so deeply dreaded,[114] that they have been drawn even from the remote parts of the counties of Waterford and Limerick, to appear at these assemblages; and, in his account of the reception which was given to Mr. O'Connell's hypothetical menace to drive the Protestants into the sea, it was said in the warmth and hastiness of the moment, a sort of rhetorical apostrophe, not intended to go beyond mere rhetoric, but the shout, or rather the thunder of fierce voices, which was simultaneously sent back, spoke volumes of dread and danger.[115] The commission from the Marquess of Anglesey was forgotten; the *if* was forgotten; they already imagined themselves in full pursuit. Nothing was remembered but O'Connell and his hundred thousand men.

Other intimations of evil purpose Mr. Wyse has recorded as afforded at those meetings. 'When will he call us out?' was more than once heard in the streets of Clonmel, during the great provincial meeting of last August; and frequently answered with the finger on the mouth, and a significant smile and wink from the by-standers.' Thus collected, and thus disposed, one hundred and forty thousand men accompanied Mr. Lawless to the town of Ballibay; and a large military force, headed by a general whom Sir Robert Peel styled 'the bravest of the brave,' and who may be said to deserve that epithet, when discretion is not the better part of valour, waited on this mighty multitude. It has been even said that the brave commander (I mean of his majesty's forces) solicited that the great army of the Association should have free passage. Three thousand Orangemen, whose numbers were increased to five thousand, resolved to contest the passage. They had fears which brave men may entertain, but a resolution which was not to be overcome, so long as they could maintain it.[116]

I pass from the subject, because it is one on which there is a difficulty of speaking, with the necessary calmness; but I cannot leave it without affirming, that if Mr. Samuel Gray, the civilian who directed the course which the Orangemen pursued on that most eventful occasion, had not been possessed of more wisdom than the gallant general who undertook to give him advice; and if he had not, relying on the heroic resolution of the little band that assembled to guard their homes from pillage and profanation, denied any passage to a barbarous multitude, except such as they could make in the face of Protestant resistance, and over Protestant carcasses, that day would have been the beginning of evils in the north; and ferocious excesses would be, perhaps, for long years after, the curse of Ulster.[117] Whatever there was of bad or vindictive feeling would be called into action, by the communications of those whose terror had been felt in the southern districts; and as the resistance would have been spirited, the destruction would have been incalculable. Better than the general, Mr. Gray knew this; and he is well entitled to the praise he has received for having stopped the progress of insurrection, and for having effected his great object without the commission of a single excess by which his triumph could be tarnished.[118]

The expedition of Mr. Lawless failed; the North was not to be terrified; perhaps it might be agitated. An agitator was announced to enact his part in Dungannon.[119] The Orange lodges assembled to form a portion of the audience, and he found it expedient to depart. No performance. He appeared in Armagh; but the Orangemen also appeared; another disappointment. Did any excess mar their triumphs? Not the slightest. No, nor the slightest ill-will; not even personal dislike to the learned individual whose operations were thus peacefully impeded. On the contrary, he is well esteemed by many Orangemen, and has, on more than one occasion, successfully, and to their great satisfaction, been employed as counsel on their behalf. But they knew the perilous consequences of agitation; they saw them in the state of the south; and while they never interfered to prevent assemblages, or processions, or commemorations of the Roman Catholics amongst whom they lived, they were resolved that the spirit of Munster disturbances should not be free to introduce its sanguinary code, and its discipline of assassination."[120]

Thus it was that the spirit of the Orange system prevented a catastrophe which would, I venture to assert, have converted the North into a sea of blood. Had the system not been at that time in active operation, the Protestants would not have had that sense of conscious strength which enabled them present a bold front to the audacious invaders; nor could those invaders have been inspired with the salutary dread and terror that laid hold upon them, by anything short of the spirit and the determination which animated the gallant band who were resolved to dispute with them the Thermopylæ of Protestant Ireland.[121] Mr. Lawless and his multitude, accordingly, retired, and the North was left in peace. He is, himself, a man full of personal courage, and I am sure he does not want its usual concomitant, humanity. Therefore I am ready to believe that he is himself rejoiced at the issue of that expedition, and would have been one of the first to deplore the excesses to which it might have led; but for their prevention he is indebted not more to his own prudence, than to the vigilance and the valour of the Orangemen of Ireland.

Nor was the firmness of this body more remarkable than their moderation. They were well content with their peaceful triumph. The assailants were suffered to go their way, unmolested by even a menace or an insult. The brave Orangemen were satisfied with acting the part of faithful and steady sentinels, and retired quietly to their domestic avocations, as soon as they had witnessed the departure of the myriads whose insulting approach threatened them with so much danger. They were mindful of the end of their organization, which was defence and not aggression; and while they felt additional cause for glorying in the bond of brotherhood, by which they were then enabled to withstand such formidable assailants, they also felt that their character might be compromised, and their triumph tarnished, if they indulged in any reprisals. It is, therefore, to their organization, and the peculiar constitution of their society, we must ascribe not only the energy and the courage which enabled them to resist popish aggression, but also the wisdom and the forbearance which limited their resistance to self-defence, and reconciled their feelings as Orangemen, when in a state of the very highest excitement, with their duty as good subjects.

The truth is, that the state of the country caused a vast accession of the loyalty, the wealth, and the respectability of the country to the Orange Institution. The very humblest of its members felt proud of a bond of connection by which they were brought into brotherly union with the very highest and the noblest in the land; and there was a natural anxiety on their part not to prove unworthy of such a distinction. They were, therefore, cautious, not only for their own sakes, but for the sake of the order to which they belonged, to avoid every act of intemperance which might cause their body to be "evil spoken of;" and it may be safely affirmed, that many of them might, as individuals, have been led into a violence of opposition to Roman Catholics, from which, as Orangemen, they were restrained. Their enemies (whose insulting and savage malevolence has been manifested almost in the same degree in which it was without the shadow of excuse) have often imputed to them crimes and atrocities which were alike abhorrent to their principles and feelings; but it has almost invariably turned out, not only that these were not the work of Orangemen, but that, had the individuals engaged in them been Orangemen, they never would have been committed. It has, however, suited the purposes of a desperate and dangerous faction to accumulate upon the heads of this constitutional body a load of imputations, which, if the truth were known, should have been shared between themselves and such unorganized Protestants as were liable to be provoked by their violence, or wrought upon by their delusions.

It is a well-known fact, that, in many instances, threatening notices have been served upon individuals, as if by Orangemen, which were only intended to bring that body into suspicion and disesteem, and which, in reality, proceeded from the opposite party.

At Lord Mulgrave's first visit to the theatre, a vast number of letters were despatched to individual Protestants and Orangemen, calling upon them to attend, and make a public demonstration of their hostility to the present government. But the forgeries were, almost in every instance detected, and this "weak invention of the enemy" failed to produce any other effect than that of putting the loyal party on their guard against them.[122]

The late affair at Belfast, on the twelfth of July, is another case in point. A triumphal arch was erected by a few poor women and boys, with whom the Orangemen were wholly unconnected. Our gallant soldiery were ordered to fire upon them, and the blood that was shed was said to have been occasioned by Orange infatuation and violence.[123] But the charge has been triumphantly refuted by the published resolutions of the Orangemen of Belfast, who had resolved not to commemorate the festival in any manner that could be construed into a violation of the law, and who defied their enemies to fasten upon any member of their body any participation in the proceedings which led to such a lamentable result. Alas! that an innocent demonstration of joy for our deliverance by King William, should have been the signal for legal murder![124]

I must, however, say, that in one respect, the Orangemen have been greatly wanting to themselves. They are without any authorised and responsible organ, by which their proceedings might be vindicated, and their principles defended. In this country they owe great obligations to the *Warder* and *Mail*; both of which papers have ever exhibited a promptitude and an ability in their cause, which should excite their gratitude and admiration. This has been done, notwithstanding that these papers have had to encounter the reproach to which the Orange system was exposed, without that degree of support from the Orangemen, as a body, to which, for such valuable assistance, they were so well entitled. The Protestant community, in general, are the patrons of our conservative journals, and the aid which they have given to the Orangemen, in particular, has often been at the risque of compromising themselves with the general reader; and while this should enhance such services in the estimation of those for whom they were wrought, it should also impress upon them the necessity of providing, in some more certain, efficacious, and permanent manner, for the only species of advocacy by which they can now hope to defeat the malice and to triumph over the wickedness of their enemies.

Nothing can now withstand a general conspiracy of the press; and Orangemen may be well convinced that the wounds which their institution has received can only be healed by a weapon somewhat similar to that by which they have been inflicted.

But there are many who may say, the Orange Institution was certainly necessary in its origin, and has been justified by its effects. It neutralized the virus of rebellion in 1798, and counteracted the machinations of treason in 1803. But is it, at present, necessary? Has not the time arrived when it may do more harm than good, or when, at least, its organization may be dispensed with?

I must, in candour, answer — no. The very same spirit now exists which necessitated its origin, and the very same practices are now to be opposed, by which its principles were justified, and its organization rendered indispensible. Indeed, the only difference is, that the disloyal party have now got more power, and ostentatiously identify themselves with the government of the country.[125]

When John Knox was accused, before the Scottish council, of recommending what was called an extraordinary meeting of the brethren, he defended his conduct by former precedents, by which, if he were then guilty, the conduct of his judges and accusers could not be justified. "Nay," said Secretary Maitland, "then was then, and now is now." "I see no difference," rejoined the intrepid reformer, "between then and now, except that now the devil has got a visor upon his face. Before he came in open tyranny, and then, I think that you will allow, the brethren rightfully assembled themselves in defence of their lives. Now he comes after another manner, seeking by cunning and artifice to do that which he could not accomplish in his own strength." The effect was electrical; the council were struck dumb; the people were excited to an active resistance to meditated oppression, and they never put off the harness until they accomplished the Scottish reformation.[126]

The case is somewhat different with us. When the Orange Institution arose, the wolf wore sheep's clothing, and it was under this disguise that he hoped to be able to ravage the flock. He was defeated and humbled; and in his defeat and humiliation there were some who saw grounds for expecting such a mitigation of his ferocity as should render him no longer dangerous. He was too cunning not to encourage this delusion, and is now fain to expect credit for the tenderest concern for those whom he meditates to make his victims. But he has thrown off disguise he appears in his native character — and, whoever else may be deceived, the Orangemen do not believe that he has changed his nature. Shall they, therefore, remit precaution because he has thrown off disguise, and is now, in some sort, a favourite with those who ought to be their natural protectors. Forbid it, common sense! They must know full well that his hostility is still as unmitigated as ever, and that when they before contended with him, they contended for supremacy; but the contest now is a contest for existence.

No one can be blind to the coming contest. Popery is again struggling for ascendency in this country, and that with greater advantages than she possessed at any former time. How is she to be resisted? By pulverising the Protestant union? By disuniting and dispersing her adversaries, so that individually they can be of no avail? No; but by reinvigorating their combination, by holding before them the adage of the bundle of sticks, and thus causing them to be consolidated into impregnable bodies, and scattered like masses of granite over the surface of the country, instead of existing like so many heaps of sand.[127]

And small must be his knowledge of human nature who does not know that, if they be not formed into combinations of one kind, they will be formed into combinations of another; that if they be not zealously for the institutions of the country, they will be zealously against them. Politically, as well as physically, large masses attract in proportion to their magnitude; and nothing but the Orange confederacy prevents a vast number of Protestants being absorbed with that portentous conspiracy which, under the pretence of a repeal of the union, meditates the dismemberment of the empire.[128] There are many considerations lying upon the surface which would be quite sufficient to swell the ranks of O'Connell's followers, if a counteracting agency had not been brought into play, which more than suffices to impair their influence. The repeal of the union is a national object, and might, upon that ground alone, be made to assume a most plausible aspect. England has abandoned her garrison;[129] and there are many who might say, and some who might think, that it is no longer either wise or patriotic to keep up the cry of "No Surrender." The church has been all but deposed — she has been rifled and mutilated, and that under the direction of a British parliament, bound by the most sacred obligations to cherish and preserve her.[130] These are topics upon which the advocates of repeal might loudly expatiate. They might point to her murdered clergy — her desecrated churches — her proscribed and persecuted people,[131] some of them in exile, others preparing to follow, while those whose destiny condemns them still to linger in their native land, at evening say, would to God it were morning; and at morning, would to God it were evening, for very weariness of a persecuted existence. Such being the blessings of British connexion and British rule, and there being no such thing as Orange organization, what answer could they make to those who might tempt them by the bait of repeal? I know of none. The repeal project would act upon them with the fascination of the rattlesnake, and they would be either drawn by the plausibilities of the demagogue, or driven by the very recklessness of their own condition to be the pledged adherents of the worst enemies of the prosperity of Ireland and the well-being of the empire.

But Orangeism is an anti-septic to all such contagious insinuations. The Orangeman knows well, that by falling in with the views of O'Connell, he would not only be acting against the weal of England, but contributing to the establishment of a domestic despotism the most galling and ruthless that could be imposed upon his native land; and therefore he bears up under all the oppressions which he at present endures, and resists all the temptations that can be presented to him with a view to seduce him from his allegiance. This he could never do in his own strength alone. As a solitary individual, he must sink under the power, or be drawn away by the alluring plausibilities of his adversaries. But, as a member of a great and powerful confederacy, comprising in it much of the wealth, the worth, and the nobility of the land, he bids them a proud defiance; and, strong in the consciousness of a good cause, he is prepared to abide the issue without fear, "until this tyranny be overpast."[132] He cannot believe that England will always, or much longer, continue deaf to the claims, or insensible to the sufferings of her afflicted brethren in this country. Her honour and interest are both too deeply concerned, to permit, much longer, a desperate faction to practise their wicked devices for our undoing; and he is thus encouraged to persevere in a righteous resistance to the oppressors, in the sure and certain hope that, however they may be defeated for a time, his constitutional exertions must be ultimately successful. But let Orangeism be put down — let its lodges be broken up, and its members scattered abroad, and nothing remains to give him confidence and courage in the contest in which he is called upon to engage, while everything must tend to deceive or to dishearten him, until he insensibly becomes either the victim or the accomplice of the enemies of Protestantism and of the constitution. From this consummation, so devoutly to be deprecated, he is saved by the protective influence of this much-calumniated institution. It operates like a species of political vaccination, and supersedes, by a mild and wholesome constitutional excitement, a malady which might otherwise prove dangerous, if not deadly. Let it be dispensed with, and the virus of the political poison will soon manifest itself with a force and a malignity that cannot be resisted.

The great offence of the Orange Institution, in the eyes of those who desire its overthrow, is, that it affords a purchase, as it were, to the maintainers of sound, conservative principles, by which the throne and the altar have hitherto been preserved against the daring assaults of unscrupulous assailants. It gives a unity and consistency, a steadiness and a force, to the efforts of the friends of social order, similar to that which political unions and reform associations have given to its enemies.[133] Therefore they wish it destroyed, that they may proceed in their work of demolition without disturbance; for they can apprehend but little interruption from the isolated efforts of scattered individuals. Now, when it is considered that the reform mania is as natural to politicians in their nonage, as the teething fever is to children of two or three years old, it is scarcely necessary to employ any artificial stimulants for its production. It is inevitably incidental to the crude state of their political knowledge, however it may be modified by the peculiarity of their tempers, or the character of their minds. A jealousy of rank, an apprehension of tyranny, a love of popular distinction, a disposition to spy out defects and to exaggerate evils in the existing order of things; these all be long to that restless, busy, meddling race of men who constitute the class denominated reformers. There needs no especial pains to excite the elements of discontent, which are always found in sufficient abundance, amidst an ignorant and an indigent population; but the contrary of all this, namely, a love of order, a respect for dignities, a veneration for established institutions, a clear perception of the difference between change and improvement, and a lively horror of the proceedings of those who, under the pretext of reform; would destroy; these are not feelings or sentiments to which men in general are naturally prone; and therefore it is the more necessary that they should be embodied in clubs and associations, having for their object the propagation of that sound political knowledge by which the machinations of the demagogue and the incendiary might be defeated. There being, then, a natural tendency to such combinations as are unconstitutional, and which may be productive of evil, and a natural indisposition to such combinations as are constitutional, and which may be productive of good, upon what plea of policy can we discourage the latter while we encourage the former; and why should Orangeism be repressed, while political unions are promoted?

It is very easy to understand why the destructives are opposed to an institution which must offer to their designs such serious obstructions; it is very easy to understand why papists should hate an institution which, as long as it exists, will not suffer the love of Protestantism to wax cold; it is very easy to understand why Orangemen should incur the peculiar detestation of the advocates of a repeal of the union. All these classes must be possessed by an instinctive antipathy towards them, as the great, if not the only obstacle to the attainment of the ends upon which they are severally bent. But, that loyal and enlightened men should so far fall in with the views of their enemies as to entertain distrust or aversion towards a body of individuals, associated as the Orangemen are, upon the strictest principles of self-defence, and for the maintenance of social order, argues, in my mind, a kind of mental alienation. It resembles the conduct of the idiot traveller who put the drag on his carriage when it was going up the hill, and took it off when it was going down. Conservative feelings and principles are, as it were, hot-bed plants which require to be cherished; their opposites resemble weeds which require to be repressed. And there are those who call themselves conservative statesmen at the present day, who seem bent upon destroying the best nurseries of the former, while no pains are taken to check the latter, which are suffered to flourish with a rank luxuriance. It is painful to contemplate the possible consequences of this political infatuation.

But, while it is acknowledged that the Orange system was originally well-intended, and that it has served very important ends, it has been asked, may it not also be powerful for evil? I answer not, without such a departure from its principles as must completely change its nature. Loyalty is its end and aim, the pole-star by which it is guided; and when it ceases to be loyal, it ceases to be Orange, and must die a natural death before it can appear in any other form from which disloyal and seditious results might be apprehended. The church might as well be charged with propagating irreligion, the courts of law with corrupting justice, the medical profession with being injurious to the public health, as the loyal association of Orangemen with entertaining designs subversive of the constitution. It is rather amusing, too, to see the class of persons whose fears have been excited lest it should become disloyal. Mr. O'Connell and Mr. Sheil are the individuals who, in their prophetic horror of future evil, recommend its extinction, notwithstanding that it might be proved to be of some present advantage. But they may calm their fears; Orangemen will never realize their wild anticipations. Their drafts upon the future will be dishonoured, even as their imputations respecting the past have been disproved. When a Roman Catholic association may be formed, friendly to the [Established] church, then they may be found hostile to it; when the repealers have changed their views and principles, and entered into a confederacy for the confirmation and establishment of the act of union, then they may be opposed to that measure, and do all in their power to have it dissolved; but not until then; so that the great agitator and his accomplices may spare themselves the pain of speculating upon impossibilities. Orange men will not be found traitors to their principles until rivers run back to their sources, or mountains invade the dominion of the sea. Mr. O'Connell may continue to believe that the same spirit which actuates them now, will continue to actuate them in all succeeding times, and that no future demagogue will ever be more successful than he has himself proved, in his attempts to seduce them from their allegiance.

The Volunteers have been mentioned as a case in point, to show that a society, originally praiseworthy and patriotic, may eventually become injurious to the public weal.[134] But the analogy does not hold; for the Volunteers were, from the first, animated by not a little jealousy of England, which only manifested itself more and more in proportion as they felt their strength; so that they but followed the law of their nature when they ultimately assumed that formidable attitude which menaced the empire with so much peril. But the Orange Institution is founded upon an affectionate attachment to British connexion, and they would be contradicting the law of their nature if they were ever betrayed into any course of action by which that connexion might be endangered. Indeed it may be said, that the acknowledged evil of the one confederacy may have, in some degree, occasioned the other. The volunteer association acted as a kind of hot-bed of discontent, in which a premature and preternatural vigour was given to the pestilent products of infidelity and sedition. It was the parent of the united Irish system. The Orange association arose for the purpose of counteracting the evils thus occasioned; and unless we apply the homoeopathic principle to politics, and maintain, that whatever will cure treasonable practices will also cause them, it will be impossible, with any degree of consistency, to maintain, that consequences such as flowed from the old volunteer system can ever be apprehended from the Orange association. At all events, it will be time enough, when such consequences do follow, to provide against them. Practical good is not to be prevented, because knaves pretend, or visionaries imagine, that they can foresee speculative evils. It is quite possible that the system of freemasonry may yet be turned to a bad account; but is it, therefore, to be suppressed at present? No one will say so. Why? Because experience has hitherto proved that it is innocuous;— and no sane politician will prefer theory to experience. In like manner, I say, let us judge of the Orange system from what all may know, not from what its enemies may choose to conjecture, and there is no individual, whose common sense has not been woefully perverted by faction, who could for one moment maintain, that a tree which has hitherto borne wholesome fruit should be cut down, because it may, at some future period, altogether change its nature, and produce most deadly poison.

There is another ground upon which the continuance of the Orange Institution may be contended for, arising out of the changes which have lately taken place in the constitution of England.[135] No one will deny that it has become vastly more democratic than it was before. The Reform Bill has thrown the governing power of the country into the hands of the people. We still have a sovereign, and we still have a House of Lords; but everyone knows that they are now regarded as but slender obstacles to the popular will, whenever it is strongly manifested; and, that if we are still to have even the semblance of a mixed government, it can only be by educating and informing the people, so as to show them the dangers which must attend its overthrow, and impress them with a grateful sense of the blessings which they have hitherto derived from its protection. That there are elements of mischief at work to produce a contrary effect; that there are individuals in whose judgment a republican form of government is preferable, and who are continually holding forth America as the model which we should seek to imitate; that there are others whose insane cupidity would lead them to desire a scramble, and who, for a little present gain or distinction, would have no objection to encounter the horrors of the French revolution, needs but to be stated to be admitted by every candid man who has paid any attention to public affairs. And, if the designs of these persons are to be resisted, they can be alone effectually resisted by a constitutional party, arising amongst the people themselves, and bent upon the promotion of constitutional objects. A strong government might dispense with such a party. Where the seditious man might be summarily coerced, it might not be quite indispensable that his pretexts should be stripped of their plausibility, and exposed in their native deformity. When the law might promptly curb his envenomed virulence, it might not be so necessary to detect his flagitious falsehood. But, no one can expect any such vigour on the part of government as at present constituted, without entertaining the most vain and chimerical expectations. The incendiaries have now a voice in the cabinet; and Hume, and Roebuck, and O'Connell, and Whittle Harvey, are sufficiently powerful to beard a conservative, and to dictate terms to an anti-conservative administration. It is, therefore, indispensable, if even the shadow of our limited monarchy is still to be preserved, that every means should be taken for cherishing whatever amount of good principle exists amongst the people at large, as the only available force that can be employed for averting the open and the secret designs of those who are preparing, as it were, an infernal machine, which they are sooner or later resolved to discharge against the constitution.[136]

It is my belief, that the force of good principle is still sufficient to defeat the force of bad, and that if we are only true to ourselves, our enemies will have no advantage over us. We need not seek for coercive laws, nor have recourse to any act of extra-constitutional rigour, in order to confound their devices. But we cannot safely dispense with any one of the means within our power for increasing, concentrating, and invigorating that attachment to the ancient institutions of the country, which is the only available antagonist to the hostility by which they are assailed. Such attachment exists to a degree of which the enemies of our institutions have no conception; even many of their friends do not know its extent. Let it be wisely employed, and all will yet be well. Let it be neglected, or undervalued, or discouraged, and nothing human can save us. In this latter case, a triumphant ascendancy will be speedily given to the powers of evil. The reign of anarchy will have commenced. A few honest and intrepid men, may, here and there, continue a hopeless struggle; but they cannot, in this unassisted struggle, long sustain the torrent that will rush against them, and in which the monarchy, the church, the House of Lords, the aristocracy, all that gives its peculiar, ennobling, and conservative character to British society, must share a common destruction.

As I stated before, the topics are upon the surface, which induce men to range themselves on the one side. Not so those which would induce them to range themselves on the other. The "movement" party aptly designates those who but follow the natural bias of their political temperament, when they recklessly pursue changes having for their object the more complete ascendancy of the democratic principle in all our civil institutions. There are, no doubt, many who are sincerely persuaded that such ascendancy is, abstractedly, desirable; and who, therefore, must be allowed to be actuated by honest motives in the course which they pursue; but the great strength, nevertheless, of that party consists in its adherents of doubtful principle; of men who intend one thing, while they pretend another; of gamblers in the lottery of politics, who are willing to stake the public good for the chance of such a prize as may gratify their personal ambition; of Dissenters, who hate the Church more than they love religion; of economists, to whom the corn laws are an offence; of infidels, to whom an ecclesiastical establishment is a crying evil; of papists, to whom a reformed Church is an abomination; of republicans, to whom a monarchical form of government must be distasteful. All these are willing to sink their differences, and to conspire for one common object. Now, the views and the motives which would lead men to make a vigorous opposition to this powerful party, do not lie upon the surface, but must be sought out and investigated, in order to be discovered and appreciated. It is not his natural inclination which will lead any one to abjure a large share of popular power, or to deny to the order to which he belongs increased influence in the affairs of the country. He can only be induced thus to act from an enlightened conviction, that, by any other course, the general harmony of society would suffer greater detriment than he or his particular class could reap advantage; and that conviction can only be acquired by a patient study of history, and in attentive observation of human affairs.

Besides, the maintainers and improvers of our institutions must be united upon many points, while those who impugn them need be united but on one. So that there is, in every balanced state, a natural combination, founded upon a kind of instinctive compromise of particular differences, always going on against the monarchical and the aristocratical institutions; while it can only be resisted by the desultory efforts of enlightened individuals, who must be always too few and too feeble to countervail their numerous and eager assailants. What then is to be done? Manifestly to form a combination, in which the friends of social order may be able effectually to propagate their convictions. If this be done, they will very soon find that good principles will not long want steady and zealous supporters. There are many, who could never themselves, hit upon ready answers to the plausibilities of the demagogue, to whom the proceedings of that character must be odious; and these will readily fall under the influence of those able men by whom his sophistries may be exposed. There are many whose love for the church is strong, but who have not themselves been able to see the fallacies involved in the attacks of its enemies. These will, naturally, be delighted to range themselves under those able champions by whom it may be defended. Thus, a party will be created by whom a popular resistance will be made to measures of a dangerously innovating character; and, without any undue departure from the forms or the usages of a free government, the balance of the constitution may be preserved. Whereas, without it, the overwhelming influence of democracy must be speedily felt; and the government of the country, no matter by whom it may be conducted, will be exposed to a succession of virulent attacks, which must end either in its overthrow or its degradation.

The reader will see at once that this great purpose has been abundantly answered by the Orange institution in Ireland. It has collected and concentrated the loyalty of the country, so that the government were always able to command abundance of assistance, whenever the aid of loyal men was required. This was felt when rebellion raged in 1798. It was also felt in 1803, when the culpable supineness of the Irish executive, almost betrayed the government into the hands of a few contemptible insurgents.[137] I remember well the confusion which prevailed at the Castle, when the Orangemen came from all quarters desiring arms and ammunition, and none were to be found! No; I am wrong. There were discovered, after a diligent search, some muskets, and some few rounds of ball cartridge; but it was found upon trial that the bore of the muskets was too small for the size of the balls!

All this may be allowed; but still it may be contended that the deficiency to which I allude may be better supplied by Conservative associations. I think not; and I think experience is with me. If by conservative associations be meant, those clubs and confederacies to which great political exigencies have given rise, they depend too exclusively upon excitement, to furnish such a steady and permanent counterpoise to the democratic faction as the case requires. It is the nature of most factions to be aggressive; and if, in one shape, it be defeated today, it will be in the field in another shape tomorrow. It possesses a kind of Protean versatility in the multiplicity and variety of the efforts which it makes for the accomplishment of its object. Without, therefore, the most unceasing vigilance, the counter agent will be in vain possessed of powers of the most vigorous resistance. Conservative associations are, I know, capable of sudden and violent efforts, by which a great deal may be done for repressing the audacity of democratic ambition. But they are also liable to be as suddenly remitted; and thus, what was gained at Cannæ may be lost at Capua,[138] and our very security of success may be the cause of our failure, and convert an humbled into a triumphant and insulting enemy. How often have I seen conservative associations arise, and flourish, and decay; leaving no more trace of what they had been, than the skyrocket leaves in the air through which it cleaves its fiery way — as brilliant as noisy, and as evanescent — alike commencing in fire, and alike concluding in smoke! Was it not thus with the Brunswick Society?[139] Was it not thus with the various other societies which, under different names, appeared from time to time, to champion the cause of our menaced institutions? And in thus going, one by one, "to the tomb of all the Capulets," they but shared the fate of every irregular and desultory effort to resist a permanent evil.[140] It may operate as a palliative, but it will not work a cure; and by disguising the malignity of the complaint, may cause the remedy to be deferred until the disease has become desperate.

The evil to be guarded against is, the tendency to continual deterioration which belongs, almost of necessity, to every system of policy in which the democratic element largely prevails. This can never be effectually met by societies which are only called into existence by its occasional extraordinary manifestations. The remedy must be as searching as the disease is deeply seated, and will never be effectual, unless it be persevered in as a sweetener and a preventive long after every apparent symptom has been removed.

Democracy is an encroaching principle, which never will rest satisfied with the limits within which it is confined. It must be restrained within them, or it will pass beyond them. Now, this necessitates either constant control, or continual resistance; and, in either case, a spirit must be called into action which will neither slumber nor sleep, so long as the arch enemy is vigilant and wakeful. Otherwise, like Aaron's rod when it became a serpent, it will speedily make an end of all its competitors.[141]

Conservative societies have always seemed to me like the seed sown upon stony places. For a time they appeared to flourish. But they took no root amongst the bulk of the people; and they were consequently doomed to barrenness and decay. But the Orange society did take root amongst the bulk of the people, and its beginnings were not more unpromising than its progress has been extraordinary. It had its origin amongst the humblest of the peasantry, and it now embraces within its association the highest and the noblest in the land. The one depended upon excitement. It could subsist only under the stimulus of extraordinary eloquence, or the provocation of formidable hostility; and, upon the withdrawal of either, a collapse was inevitable. The other depended upon principle. It had, as it were, its peace establishment and its war establishment. When the enemy was absent, it was vigilant; when he was present, it was prepared.

Therefore it is, that in my humble judgment, the Orange association is infinitely preferable, for combining all good men in the unity of sound political faith, to any other with which I am acquainted. It is like one of those spontaneous productions which nature furnishes in such abundance where poisons grow, and which are intended as an antidote. Not to speak profanely, I do fervently believe it to have been providentially provided, for the purpose of counteracting evils which the nature of our political position necessitated, and which no human sagacity could have foreseen or averted. It strengthened the hands of the executive when the crown itself was tottering under the assaults of faction; and in the midst of treason, it caused a spring tide of loyalty to set in amongst the people, by which conspirators were dismayed and confounded. When popish bigotry and cruelty, taking advantage of our political insecurity, were about, again, to manifest themselves in their accustomed atrocities and abominations, the Orange institution, like Aaron of old, stood between the living and the dead, and the plague was stayed.[142] It is, therefore, impossible for the wise and good not to feel grateful for services such as these, even as it is impossible for those whose wicked devices were thus frustrated, not to feel hatred for an institution but for which their bloody and destructive projects might long ago have been successful.

And it is melancholy to perceive that gratitude is evanescent, while hatred is eternal. How aptly, at the present day, do O'Connell and Sheil represent the old enmity by which Orangemen were regarded in 1798? But where, at the present day, are we to find any adequate representation of the gratitude of which they were the objects, when they were pronounced the saviours of their country? Alas! Echo answers, "where!" But I do not despond. Far from it. I said I believe the institution to have been providentially designed. That is, in fact, my ground of hope. I see that it has performed great service for Ireland heretofore. I think that it will still triumph over its secret and its open enemies, and perform still greater service for the British empire.

There is one especial feature of the institution which has called forth the bitterest and the most contemptuous revilings. That is, that every meeting of every lodge is opened and closed with prayer.[143] It is perfectly impossible for anyone who has not witnessed it, to conceive the effect which this practice has on the spirit that pervades their deliberations. A degree of seriousness, solemnity, and sanctity, is thus imparted, which more than anything else has contributed to keep sacred principle alive, and to feed the vestal flame of loyalty, by which the devoted watchers keep guard at the gate of the constitution.[144] It is no wonder that Mr. Hume should have constructions fastened upon it, as a practice deserving HIS weightiest reprobation[145] — for it is, no doubt, most disagreeable to the master whom he serves; and he were unworthy the distinction that master has enabled him to attain, if he did not bear his decided testimony against it.[146] But not the less, I trust, will it continue to distinguish those whom he has honoured with his vituperation, and who would have reason to feel that they forfeited the Divine favour, if they were so unfortunate as to incur his praise.

The very fact of being able to commence and conclude their meetings in the manner they do, implies the consciousness of a good purpose. He that doeth evil cometh not unto the light, lest his deeds should be reproved; but every one that doeth good cometh to the light, that his deeds may be made manifest that they are wrought in God.[147] These words are not profaned when applied to the feelings and principles of Orangemen, who could not, cherishing any latent evil in their hearts, any envy, hatred, malice, or uncharitableness, use a form of prayer which could only, in such a case, be mockery the most gratuitous and revolting. Supposing them bad men, their meetings are secret meetings, they are not of the character of those which were held in synagogues, or in the corners of streets, where they might have their reward in receiving the praise of men. Each other they could not deceive, and there was no one else upon whom deception could be possibly practised. Why, then, persevere in an observance, in which hypocrisy was not only profitless but impracticable? The notion is absurd. No sane enemy of the institution could, for a moment, entertain it. It remains, then, that their prayers are uttered in sincerity. And let anyone who can read them with an understanding heart, and conceive them in an honest spirit, judge whether or no those by whom they are habitually adopted, are conscious of rectitude in their intentions.

But these prayers have given offence to Mr. Joseph Hume. The reader will remember that he was scandalized at the acknowledgment of an overruling Providence, and he will not be surprised that the simple piety of the Orangemen fell under his reprobation. But not the less, do I trust, that they will persevere in it; and I desire no other answer to be given to it from on high, than that efficacy which has hitherto attended their labours. It is impossible that it should not serve to impress upon the minds of Orangemen a due sense of their deep and sacred obligations. If there should be offenders found amongst them, (as what so extensive society can be wholly free from them,) let them spare no pains to correct and to reclaim them. And should they prove incorrigible, let them be unhesitatingly cast out from amongst the brethren. Thus alone can they themselves be exempted from reproach. But, if all act in the spirit of those prayers, in which they commend themselves to throne of grace, it is not easy for a Christian man to believe that a divine blessing will not attend them.

This I would not so confidently affirm, if I did not know that the prayers which Orangemen use are equally free from fanaticism and coldness. They are calm and equable, while they are elevating and sublime; and are so well calculated to impress solemn thoughts upon reasonable minds, that I have heard respectable Whig gentlemen, who were only made acquainted with them by Mr. Hume's contemptuous notice of them in parliament, express their astonishment how anyone could be found in a Christian assembly so devoid of proper feeling as to treat them with disrespect, or even to refer to them without reverence.

But, there is another objection to which my favourite institution, and, indeed, all conservative or other societies, may be exposed. It may be contended that it might prove too strong for any government, and even fetter the free deliberations of parliament. From what has been already said, the reader must have perceived that there is, already, in existence, a force of faction which has proved too strong for any government which it has as yet encountered, and by which the free deliberation of parliament has been materially restricted. There is a control exercised without, which greatly cripples the liberty of those who are within the House of Commons, and which menaces, with its high displeasure, the House of Lords themselves, if they should prove refractory or disobedient. Now, supposing all societies for the promotion of sound constitutional views perfectly quiescent, are the government able to maintain their position against democratic encroachments? The objection to which I now allude is one that has been urged by Lord Stanley, in his letter to Sir Thomas Hesketh, respecting the Lancashire conservative association.[148] Lord Stanley was the man who was mainly instrumental in passing the reform bill. Without his countenance and support it never would have become the law of the land. Next to Lord Grey, he is responsible for that sweeping measure.[149] Now, if I might presume to take so great a liberty, I would respectfully ask his lordship, what stand was he himself able to make, in the newly modelled House of Commons, in favour of the Irish church? Everyone knows the power with which, in the old House of Commons, he defended it. Everyone knows the vigour with which he chastised the spoliators who meditated its destruction. Indeed in those days it was not easy to get them to commit themselves so far in their attacks upon it as fairly to justify so strong an imputation. They were like rats which merely show their noses from their holes, well knowing, that by any further exposure, their lives would be endangered. The noble lord, therefore, in his castigation of Hume and others, had comparatively easy work. The more timid of them hid their diminished heads in his presence, and the more audacious fled, howling. But what is the case, now that the noble lord has pulled up the flood gates of democracy? Have not he and the culprits whom he chastised, almost changed places? Is there now any timid disavowal of the ultimate intention of the partisans of ecclesiastical plunder?[150] Let the prostrate condition of the Irish church answer the question, and the triumphant position of its enemies in parliament. It is only saved from utter destruction by the yet unsubverted or unreformed House of Lords. And yet I will be bold to say, "Si pergama possent defendi,"[151] if such an institution could be effectually defended in such an assembly, by no one could it be more powerfully defended than by the noble lord. But he has himself so damaged the condition of that legislative body, that neither he, nor any other wise or honest man, can expect to exercise their proper and legitimate influence amongst the vain, the heady, and the reckless individuals whom it now numbers amongst its members. Until, therefore, Lord Stanley proves, that a constitutional party in the House of Commons are sufficient in themselves to oppose an effectual resistance to the dangerous spirit of innovation which is now abroad, it is too soon to talk of the danger to be apprehended from the Orange or the Conservative Associations. Whatever has as yet been done to resist that spirit, has been done chiefly through their instrumentality; and were it not for them, I doubt, exceedingly, whether, in a very few years, Lord Stanley himself could find his way into parliament.

If the noble lord really wish to do any good, (and I am one of those who most cordially admit his good intentions,) let him address himself to his friends, the radical Whigs. Let him point out the danger of their proceedings to the Birmingham union, the trades political union, the reform association, and the various other political fungi, which the diseased state of the body politic has caused to start into existence.[152] He has a natural claim upon them, seeing how much he has done for them, and how little, but for him, they could have done either for themselves or against their country. Let the noble lord expostulate with them, upon the insane violence of their conduct. But will he be listened to with attention or respect? Will any filial, or dutiful obedience be manifested by those whom he called into being? The noble lord it was who opened the windows of the heavens, and broke up the foundation of the great deep, until the country was deluged with democracy. Will the waters subside again at his command, and has he the power of confining them to their proper channels, and saying, thus far shalt thou go, and no farther?[153] Mockery and scorn would wait upon the attempt, and the noble lord would soon be made to feel the sort of gratitude to which his protégées considered him entitled. It would remind him of the predicament of Ulysses, in the den of Polyphemus.[154]

No! It is by the Conservative Societies whom Lord Stanley has opposed, that he is supported. It is by the Orangemen of Ireland, whose character he misrepresented, and whose institution he has injured, that he is held in high esteem. They have differed from him, and they must continue to differ from him, on many points of great importance. And I shall only add, that if he only knew them as well as they know him, the time, perhaps, is not very distant, when, with one mind and one heart, they would be contending together for all that remains of the constitution.

And this brings me, naturally, to that peculiar condition to which England has been reduced by the reform bill, and which renders it more necessary than ever that the Orange system should be kept up in Ireland. Coleridge well said, respecting her foreign policy of late years, that her insensibility to the disgrace which she has incurred in the eyes of all honest and thinking men, reminded him of a man, who, in consequence of a violent stimulant applied to one part of his body, was unconscious of injuries done to the other.[155] In fact, while she is, herself, struggling for existence, with a desperate faction, distant interests must be neglected. Now this applies with peculiar force to this country, in which it is the object of that desperate faction to depress and dispirit the loyal, and to sustain and encourage the disloyal portion of the people. The church is to be plundered and abandoned, and the best friends of British connection are to be systematically insulted and reviled. It may be pleaded, that England, as she is at present governed, cannot help this. Her wretched ministers are at the mercy of a popish faction who must be propitiated,[156] and they possess not the power, even if they had the inclination, to obtain better terms for the loyal Protestants of Ireland. But only so much the more, therefore, does it behove those loyal Protestants, to endeavour to secure or to obtain for themselves what cannot or will not be obtained for them by the government of the country. By a firm, peaceable, determined resistance to the desperate courses at present pursued, much may be done to delay, if not to avert, the destruction which must otherwise inevitably attend them. And how can this be better accomplished, than by means of the compact and energetic organization of the Orange Institution. It is not for brave men to strike their colours at the first appearance of formidable danger.[157] It is not for Christian men to despair of the ultimate stability of a gospel church, which, by a very little adaptation to the circumstances of the age, may be made the greatest blessing to the country. The sentiment should ever be in their hearts, "God is in the midst of her, therefore shall she not be removed; God shall help her, and that right early."[158] They should, therefore, persevere in the noble and the holy determination of leaving nothing undone on their part which may serve to expose and to defeat the crafts and assaults of the enemy. And the very embarassments [sic] of the goverment [sic] by whom they ought to be protected, should only inspire them with a more earnest desire to labour for the maintenance and the preservation of all that is valuable to them as men and as Christians. While the British ministry sympathised with them, and could, at any moment, assist them, it might not have been so indispensable to enter into combinations for the security of their religion, their properties, and their lives; and yet the reader has seen that even then, such combinations were by no means useless. How much more must it be necessary now, when, humanly speaking, it is their only resource against impending evils "until this tyranny be overpast!"[159]

And this tyranny WILL be overpast. England is every hour awaking from her democratic delusion. A day does not pass over our heads without adding to the number of those good men and true, who deplore the sufferings of, and are uniting to make common cause with their brethren in Ireland. Remember Derry.[160] Let the suffering Irish Protestant hold in mind that memorable siege, when its noble inhabitants stalked gaunt and fleshless skeletons through their beleaguered town, and when their cry was still "no surrender." We are not as yet reduced to those straits; and the same help in time of need which rescued them, may, in our extremity, be extended to us, if we are animated by their brave example.

This is the gloomy hour of Ireland. The powers of darkness have obtained a terrible ascendancy. But if we trust not in God, in such emergencies, where is our faith? And if we persevere not in in a righteous resistance to oppression and wickedness, will we not be regarded as self-abandoned? But that may not be. Our cause is a holy cause, and we cannot desert it or despair of it, without a degree of impiety that would justify the heaviest visitation. Besides, England has heard our cry, and will help us. That noble people are discovering how grossly they have been abused.[161] The murder of our clergy, the expatriation of our Protestant yeomen,[162] the attack upon our church, the insolent domination of the Roman Catholic priests, the confiscation of ecclesiastical revenues, the whole course of legislation respecting us which has been pursued in the imperial parliament, the exposures which have taken place, at Exeter Hall and elsewhere, of the infamous and uncharitable dogmas taught in Dens' Theology — all these things must have produced a conviction of the oppression under which we labour, and the ruthless tyranny to which we are in danger of being exposed, and it only requires that that conviction should be somewhat more extensive, in order to our salvation.[163]

Let us, therefore, in God's name, not be wanting to ourselves. The times, I know, are trying. Faithful men are put to a severe test. Even their notions of loyalty are against them, in a crisis like the present, rendering it difficult for them to recognize in the King's ministers the enemies of his kingdom. I do not say that these ministers are knowingly such enemies. But surely their measures are in direct hostility to what men in their position should look upon as good and right, and must tend to the overthrow of the monarchy, if they be not strenuously resisted. Resist them, therefore, we must, or perish. When I say resist, I mean, of course, constitutional resistance. We must meet them at the registries and on the hustings.[164] Above all, we must meet them by an able and energetic press. That great regulator of public opinion has been too long, by the conservative party, most unwisely neglected. To do justice to the enemies of our institution, they have not neglected it. It has been, in their hands, as a lever for the overthrow of the church and the monarchy. By its means they have already metamorphosed the constitution. But that which has been thus rendered powerful for evil may, in good hands, be made powerful for good; and if the Conservatives are true to themselves, they may employ it upon a vantage ground that would soon give them an unbounded control over the great majority of the constituencies of the empire. This I say, from my deeply-seated conviction of the moral worth and the political honesty of the people of England. In their very worst and weakest acts they clearly exhibited good intentions. They were misinformed, they were deluded, they were led astray, during the reform mania; and for this I will not say that the vile radical press were one whit more responsible than that great party by whom it was so long suffered to work its wicked will, without any effective counteraction. But so it was; the people were never more convinced of being right than when they were most grossly wrong; and they laboured with all the zeal of patriots for objects which, if they had been more correctly informed as to their nature and tendency, they would, as patriots, have abjured.

Nor is it too late to give them that sound information by which the worst evils that threaten us may yet be averted. But not a moment is to be lost. Let the statesman whose high behest it is to consult for their moral and political welfare recollect that he has not to deal with a French populace, or a Belgic populace. Let him recollect that he has not to deal with a people to whom liberty is a novelty, and of whom it might be said that "the stranger had got into their heads." The British nation were cradled in free institutions, and they have been a gospel-hearing and a Bible-reading people for three hundred years. There is, therefore, a solid ground for political faith in such a people, that is not to be found elsewhere, and the statesman who wants it at the present day cannot preside with advantage over the destinies of England. Let him only duly and diligently seek, and he will surely find, that there is no lack of that "righteousness that exalteth a nation," even though there should be no small abundance of that "sin that is a reproach to any people."[165] And under a wise and righteous administration of the powers of government he will have the satisfaction of seeing that the one will increase, while the other will decrease, until knowledge and piety will be more than a match for the infidelity and the reckless ignorance that have hitherto pioneered the progress of popular ambition.

But I must not suffer myself to be drawn from my purpose by any general dissertation on the state of affairs. My purpose was and is the defence of the Orangemen of Ireland. The reader has seen what may be said on their behalf, and it is for him to judge whether or not it ought to be considered sufficient to refute the allegations against them. Indeed I could wish to refer those who desire fuller information than I have given them to the parliamentary report of the select committee appointed to inquire into the origin, the character, and the effects of the Orange Association in Ireland. That committee was moved for by one of the bitterest enemies of the institution; and having consumed nearly the whole session in a close and scrutinizing investigation, they have been unable to fasten any other imputation on the system than that lodges have been held in marching regiments; but they were utterly unable to discover a single fact to prove that by their existence military discipline was injured.

The Orangemen will not do themselves justice unless selections from the evidence taken before that committee be collected and published, for the information of the public at large. They should be particularly careful to extract and to disseminate the admissions and the contradictions of their enemies.

I now take leave of the subject. What an old man, who may be said to have been one of those who "rocked the cradle" of the Institution, could do for it, I have done. I trust it will not be my fate to "follow its hearse." But I write under a pressure of events, which bear heavily on the fortunes of Protestant Ireland. The session has nearly closed, and the arch agitator is still enthroned in absolute supremacy over a government which, as Sir Robert Peel has well said, has accepted of office upon the condition of giving him power. The Orangemen are already denounced and proscribed. To be an Orangeman is to incur disqualification for civil or military employment. Where will this end!

> Oh! what a world is this, when what is comely
> Envenoms him that bears it![166]

But my brave and loyal brethren will, I trust, bear up, and maintain a good heart, under these insulting and injurious persecutions. Let them be assured that any violence into which they might be betrayed will only, in a tenfold degree, strengthen the hands of their enemies. Their reliance must be on their good cause, their tranquil demeanour, and the awakening good sense of the people of England. Let nothing be left undone to put that people in possession of their whole case, and to remove the prejudices which they have been taught to entertain against them, and I venture to prophesy that the day of their triumph is not very distant. Falsehood must soon vanish before correct information, and loyalty will not always be held in dim eclipse by convicted treason, and all loyal Orangemen will have the satisfaction of finding that "by a patient perseverance in well-doing they will put to shame the ignorance of foolish men."[167]

MONTANUS
County Down, Sept. 10th, 1835.

I should have said that the special committee appointed to inquire into the nature and effects of the Orange Institution terminated their labours rather abruptly. When it commenced its sittings, the accusers of the Orangemen were not prepared to go on with their case, and before any attempt was made to inculpate them by any serious charge, their advocates were called upon to prove that they were blameless. This was sufficiently preposterous. Well, accordingly, the witnesses on their behalf were summoned, and before one—half of them were examined, certainly before the Orangemen had an opportunity of putting forward one-half of their case, the committee change their minds, dismiss the witnesses, and enter upon the adverse case — upon an express understanding, however, that the gentlemen then dismissed would be recalled, and that an ample opportunity would be afforded of rebutting the charges and the allegations of their enemies. Your readers will be surprised to hear that not one of these gentlemen were recalled, and that the whole time of the committee during the remainder of the session was occupied in hearing the statements of their adversaries.

In the course of the Rev. Mortimer O'Sullivan's examination some strong points were made against the church of Rome. It did not appear, to those who heard them, altogether so incomparable and so immaculate as Mr. O'Connell usually represents it. It did not, indeed, appear wholly free from imputations of intolerance and perfidy, by which Mr. O'Connell's choler was greatly moved, insomuch that the honourable and learned gentleman offered himself as a witness, to be examined by his own committee, for the purpose of disproving the Rev. Gentleman's statements. However, in proportion as he deployed his facts, Mr. O'Connell eschewed the task of refutation, and was understood to have intimated to the chairman of the committee that he had no desire to be examined. But towards the close of the proceedings he changed his mind, and he did appear as a witness, and he was suffered to put in one or two documents, by which, as he conceived, a strong impression must be made, without any sufficient pains having been taken to test their authenticity. This strange proceeding has given rise to a letter from the Rev. Mortimer O'Sullivan, which puts the whole case in a clear light, and which must produce a powerful effect, contrasting as it does the rigidness of the scrutiny which was applied to the statements of the Orange witnesses with the easiness with which those of the opposite party were admitted. Let any impartial man, or indeed, any man of any party, read it, and then say whether he would like to have the same justice done to him which was received from the above named committee by the Orangemen of Ireland. — M.

We had intended to have transferred to our pages the admirable letter of Mr. O'Sullivan to which our correspondent alludes — not so much in the expectation that it might in this shape meet the eye of anyone who has not already read it, as from a wish to give it greater permanence than belongs to the fleeting columns of a newspaper. We regret, however, that want of space prevents us from carrying our intention into effect.

Our valued correspondent has now concluded his series of letters, and we feel persuaded that it is needless for us to express our admiration of the ability and temper with which he has supported the cause of his brethren. It is with unaffected sincerity that we say, that we feel proud that our pages have been the medium of giving to the public so eloquent and powerful a defence of the principles of Orangeism. At the same time, we are sure that our friend will excuse us if we feel it necessary to repeat our declaration, that for the opinions he has expressed we are not responsible. There are many points upon which we disagree with him. We have a much greater jealousy of extra-constitutional associations than "Montanus" entertains — we believe that nothing but imperious necessity can justify their existence; and we cannot agree with "Montanus" that this necessity is an inevitable result of the democratic element of our constitution. We think, too, that our correspondent has not given sufficient credit to the labours of the Brunswick Clubs and the Conservative Society — the latter especially performed services to the cause of Protestantism that no Protestant ever should forget. Upon these and some other points we would wish that Montanus had expressed himself differently; but we would have been unpardonable had we permitted these differences to be the cause of our withholding these excellent letters from the public.

We trust that the suggestion with regard to publishing extracts from the evidence taken before the committee will not be lost sight of. We are happy to avail ourselves of this opportunity of recording our admiration of the evidence given by the officers of the Institution, who, under the most harassing cross-examination, conducted themselves with the most perfect prudence and good temper. The evidence given by Mr. Baker and by Mr. Blacker, the Deputy Treasurer and Secretary of the Institution, is peculiarly valuable, and reflects equal credit upon the talents and discretion of these gentlemen.

Our correspondent has not alluded to the atrocious plot discovered by Mr. O'Connell and Mr. Hume, having for its object the altering of the succession to the crown — to ensure which all Orangemen were, so long as such an oath was legal, sworn to maintain that succession!![168]

We cannot conclude these few remarks without noticing the affair between the Corporation of Cork and the Privy Council. Some ragamuffins of Cork called themselves the citizens of Cork, and presented a petition against the newly-appointed Mayor, on the ground of his being an Orangeman.[169] For the resent Lord Mulgrave and his Council have withheld their approval of the election. As the matter is still pending, we will not usurp the judicial functions of the Privy Council by commenting on it. We can scarcely, however, anticipate a decision by which the Council will institute themselves into a Star Chamber, to make that a crime which the law does not, and punish a British subject for belonging to a legal society, which has only been denounced by Mr. O'Connell. If they do, farewell to British liberty — unless Britons be prepared at all extremities to preserve it. A.P.

September 21st.

Notes

Introductory Essay

1. The *DUM* had been launched in January by a group of young Trinity College Tories, 'in part to counter the new political doctrines exemplified by the 1832 Reform Bill, as well as the feelings of despair and ruin that such doctrines were now causing in Tory circles.' Wayne E. Hall, *Dialogues in the Margin: A Study of the Dublin University Magazine* (Washington DC, 1999), p. 34. It defended the privileges of the established Church of Ireland and took a great deal of interest in the antiquities and culture of Ireland.
2. Kevin Haddock-Flynn, *Orangeism: A Historical Profile* (Leicestershire, 2020), p. 202.
3. Letter From an Old Orangeman, *Dublin University Magazine*, August 1835, p. 193.
4. The classic defence of the Order is Member of the Order [R. M. Sibbett], *Orangeism in Ireland and Throughout the Empire* (London, n.d. [1939]). For more recent examples, Ruth Dudley Edwards, *The Faithful Tribe: An Intimate Portrait of the Loyal Institutions* (London: Harper Collins, 1999) and Eric Kaufmann, *The Orange Order: A Contemporary Northern Irish History* (Oxford, 2007).
5. Letter From an Old Orangeman, p. 204.
6. Second Letter From an Old Orangeman, *Dublin University Magazine*, August 1835, pp 270–7. My emphasis.
7. Ibid., p. 272.
8. Ibid., pp 273–4.
9. Ibid., p. 273.
10. Third Letter From an Old Orangeman, *Dublin University Magazine*, October 1835, p. 437.
11. Ibid., p. 430.
12. G.I.T. Machin, *The Catholic Question in English Politics, 1820 to 1830* (Oxford, 1964), pp 135–6.
13. Note the DUM's closing editorial comment of the Letters. 'We have a much greater jealousy of extra-constitutional associations than "Montanus"

entertains — we believe that nothing but imperious necessity can justify their existence; and we cannot agree with "Montanus" that this necessity is an inevitable result of the democratic element of our constitution.' Third Letter From an Old Orangeman, *Dublin University Magazine*, October 1835, p. 444.
14. Third Letter of an Old Orangeman, *Dublin University Magazine*, September 1835, p. 435.
15. Ibid., p. 432.
16. Document 11, 'Byrne's account for 1787', in David Miller (ed.), *Peep o'Day Boys and Defenders: Selected Documents on the Disturbances in County Armagh, 1784–1796* (Belfast: Public Record Office of Northern Ireland, 1990), p. 46
17. Timothy D. Watt, *Popular Protest and Policing in Ascendancy Ireland, 1691–1761* (Suffolk: Boydell & Brewer, 2018), p. 73.
18. James Mullalla, *A View of Irish Affairs Since the Revolution of 1688* (1795), p. 167.
19. Padhraig Higgins, *A Nation of Politicians: Gender, Patriotism, and Political Vulture in Late Eighteenth-Century Ireland* (Madison, WI, 2010), p. 135.
20. Evidence of Mortimer O'Sullivan, chaplain to the Orange Order, in House of Commons, *Report from the Select Committee on Orange Lodges, Associations or Societies in Ireland, ordered to be printed 20 July 1835*, p. 33.
21. Document 26: Rev. Edward Hudson to the Earl of Charlemont, 26 August 1789, in David Miller (ed.), *Peep o'Day Boys and Defenders: Selected Documents on the Disturbances in County Armagh, 1784–1796* (Belfast, 1990), p. 90.
22. Thomas Bartlett, 'Ireland during the Napoleonic and Revolutionary Wars', in *The Cambridge History of Ireland: Volume III, 1730–1880* ed. by James Kelly (Cambridge, 2018), p. 82.
23. For an account, see Richard Musgrave, *Memoirs of the Different Rebellions in Ireland*, vol II (Dublin: Robert Marchbank, 1802), pp 59–62.
24. See Kyla Madden, *Forkhill Protestants and Forkhill Catholics, 1787–1858* (Ithaca: McGill-Queen's University Press, 2005), pp 156–157
25. R. H. Wallace, 'History of the Orange Order: The formative years, 1795–1798', in *The Formation of the Orange Order, 1795–1798: The Edited Papers of Colonel William Blacker and Colonel Robert H. Wallace* (Belfast: Education Committee of the Grand Orange Lodge of Ireland, 1994), p. 78.
26. Laurence's Trial for High Treason, *The Register of the Times*, vol. VI (London, 1795) p. 325.
27. Bartlett, '"Second digest of intelligence received by government respecting Defenderism": Select Documents XXXVIII: Defenders and Defenderism in 1795', in *Irish Historical Studies*, 24: 95 (1985), p. 392.

28. Patrick Tohall, 'The Diamond fight of 1795 and the resultant expulsions', in *Seanchas Ardmhacha: Journal of the Armagh Diocesan Historical Society*, 1958, 3: 1 (1958), pp 17–22.
29. Hereward Senior, *Orangeism in Ireland and Britain, 1795–1836* (London, 1966), p. 18.
30. Member of the Order [R. M. Sibbett], *Orangeism in Ireland and Throughout the Empire*, vol. I (London, n.d. [1939]), p. 285.
31. Wallace, 'History of the Orange Order: The formative years, 1795–1798', p. 67.
32. William Blacker, 'The Battle of the Diamond' [1836] in *The Formation of the Orange Order, 1795–1798: The Edited Papers of Colonel William Blacker and Colonel Robert H. Wallace* (Belfast, 1994), p. 19.
33. Appendix VI, 'Meeting of the Magistrates of Armagh, 28 December 1795', in Edward Hay, *History of the Irish Insurrection of 1798* (New York, 1803, 1847), p. 402.
34. Hereward Senior, *Orangeism in Ireland and Britain, 1795–1836* (London, 1966), p. 18, 30, 37. Francis Plowden, *Historical Disquisition Concerning the Orange Societies in Ireland* (Dublin, 1810), pp 66–7.
35. Sir Lawrence Parsons in a speech to the House of Commons in 1796, *Report from the Select Committee on Orange Lodges, Associations or Societies in Ireland, ordered to be printed 20 July 1835*, p. 332.
36. R. B. McDowell, *Irish Public Opinion, 1750–1800* (London, 1943), pp 239–40.
37. Ibid., *Ireland in the Age of Imperialism and Revolution, 1760–1801* (Oxford, 1979, 1991), p. 475.
38. Member of the Order [R. M. Sibbett], *Orangeism in Ireland and Throughout the Empire*, vol. I (London, n.d. [1939]), p. 357.
39. Ibid., p. 329.
40. See 'Orange Marksmen' membership requirements cited in Hereward Senior, *Orangeism in Ireland and Britain, 1795–1836* (London, 1966), p. 78. Wallace writes that 'many of the earlier initiations were performed behind hedges or in dry ditches, which originated the nicknames "hedgers" and "ditchers"'. Wallace, 'History of the Orange Order: The formative years, 1795–1798', p. 48.
41. Knox to Lake, 18 March 1798, in W. E. H. Lecky, *A History of England in the Eighteenth Century*, vol. VII (London, 1890), p. 312.
42. Hereward Senior, *Orangeism in Ireland and Britain, 1795–1836* (London: Routledge & Kegan Paul, 1966), p. 83.
43. [Sibbett], *Orangeism in Ireland and Throughout the Empire*, p. 428.
44. Cornwallis to Ross, 24 July 1798, in Cornwallis, *Correspondence*, II, p. 369.

45. Allan Blackstock, *Loyalism in Ireland, 1789–1829* (Woodbridge: Boydell, 2007), p. 103. See also, Letter from Lord Masserene to the Lord Lieutenant, 28 May 1803, complaining that former 'hierarchs of the Union bands' had been admitted into the Yeomanry in Antrim. A. W. P. Malcomson (ed.), *The Extraordinary Career of the 2nd Earl of Masserene, 1745–1805: Select Documents* (Belfast, 1972), p. 101.
46. Hereward Senior, *Orangeism in Ireland and Britain, 1795–1836* (London: Routledge & Kegan Paul, 1966), p. 133.
47. According to affidavits, sixty-eight loyalists were massacred in Wicklow, and about 450 in Wexford. Edward Baines, *History of the Wars of the French Revolution*, vol. I (London, 1818), p. 244
48. Second Letter From an Old Orangeman, *Dublin University Magazine*, September 1835, p. 271.
49. David Fitzpatrick, *Descendancy: Irish Protestant Histories Since 1795* (Cambridge: Cambridge University Press, 2014), p. 28.
50. John Mogey, 'Social relations in rural society', in T. W. Moody and J. C. Beckett, *Ulster Since 1800: A Social Survey: Second Series* (London, 1957), p. 73.
51. Lady Gregory (ed.), *Mr. Gregory's Letter-Box, 1813–1830* (London, 1898), p. 93.
52. 'Origins of the Ribbon Men', *The Orthodox Journal, and Catholic Monthly Intelligencer*, vols 1–2 (1813), p. 39. See also Robert Huish, *The Memoirs, Private and Political, of Daniel O'Connell* (London: W. Johnson, 1836), pp 300–1.
53. Second Letter From an Old Orangeman, *Dublin University Magazine*, September 1835, p. 274.
54. House of Commons, 9 June 1814, col. 36.
55. M. W. Dewar, John Brown, S. E. Long, *Orangeism: A New Historical Appreciation*, 2nd edn, p. 118.
56. Quoted in Sean Farrell, *Rituals and Riots: Sectarian Violence and Political Culture in Ulster, 1784–1886* (Lexington, 2000), p. 75.
57. *Belfast Magazine*, September 1814, pp 231–2.
58. House of Commons, *A Digest of the Evidence in the First Report from the Select Committee on the State of Ireland* (London, 1825), p. 187.
59. [Sibbett], *Orangeism in Ireland and Throughout the Empire* and Farrell, *Rituals and Riots, passim.*
60. Hereward Senior, *Orangeism in Ireland and Britain, 1795–1836* (London, 1966), p. 110.
61. Thomas Reid, *Travels in Ireland in the Year 1822* (London, 1823), p. 193.
62. David Dickson, *Dublin: The Making of a Capital City* (London, 2014), p. 301.

63. H. W. Cleary, *The Orange Society* (London, 1899), p. 348.
64. Kevin Haddock-Flynn, *Orangeism: A Historical Profile* (Leicestershire, 2020), pp 183–4.
65. Sir Spencer Walpole, *A History of England from the Conclusion of the Great War in 1815* (London, 1880), p. 339.
66. W. Torrens McCullagh, *Memoirs of the Right Honourable Richard Lalor Sheil*, vol. II (London, 1855), p. 27.
67. Denis Carolan Rushe, *Historical Sketches of Monaghan* (Dublin, 1895), p. 85.
68. Third Letter From an Old Orangeman, *Dublin University Magazine*, September 1835, p. 429.
69. Denis Carolan Rushe, *Historical Sketches of Monaghan* (Dublin, 1895), pp 86–90; *Conduct of Police Employed in Collection of Tithes in County of Monaghan 1834*, House of Commons Parliamentary Papers, (239) XLIII (1834).
70. Letter to P. V. Fitzpatrick, 1833, John Fitzpatrick (ed.), *Correspondence of Daniel O'Connell: The Liberator*, vol. I (London: John Murray, 1888), p. 326.
71. Charles Greville, *The Greville Memoirs A Journal of the Reigns of King George IV. and King William IV*, vol. II (London: Longmans, Green, 1874), p. 100.
72. Allan Blackstock, 'Tommy Downshire's Boys: Popular protest, social change and political manipulation in Mid-Ulster 1829–1847', *Past & Present*, 196 (2007), p. 142, 147.
73. Select Committee on Orange Lodges, Associations or Societies in Ireland, *Report*, Minutes of Evidence, Appendix, p. 131. For Melbourne's positive response, see Hereward Senior, *Orangeism in Ireland and Britain, 1795–1836* (London, 1966), p. 245.
74. Jay R. Roszman, *Outrage in the Age of Reform Irish Agrarian Violence, Imperial Insecurity, and British Governing Policy, 1830–1845* (Cambridge, 2022), p. 59.
75. Hereward Senior, *Orangeism in Ireland and Britain, 1795–1836* (London, 1966), p. 268.
76. Third Letter From an Old Orangeman, *Dublin University Magazine*, September 1835, p. 443.
77. Frank Wright, *Two Lands on One Soil: Ulster Politics before Home Rule* (Dublin, 1996), p. 136, 153.
78. *The Edinburgh Review*, January 1850, p. 114.
79. Ibid., p. 105.
80. Neil P. Maddox, '"A melancholy record": The story of the nineteenth-century Irish Party Processions Act', *Irish Jurist* (2004).

81. Aiken McClelland, 'The Later Orange Order' in T. Desmond Williams (ed.), *Secret Societies in Ireland* (Dublin, 1973), p. 126.
82. Alvin Jackson, 'Johnston, William (1829–1902), Orangeman', *Oxford Dictionary of National Biography* (2004).
83. See Frank Thompson, 'The Landed Classes, the Orange Order and the Anti-Land League Campaign in Ulster, 1880–1881', *Éire-Ireland*, xxii, 1 (1987).
84. A. T. Q. Stewart, *The Ulster Crisis: Resistance to Home Rule, 1912-1914* (Belfast, 1967, 1997), pp 31–2, 46–8, 63–4, 69–71.
85. *Derry Journal*, 24 July 1963.
86. John F Harbinson, *The Ulster Unionist Party, 1882–1973* (Belfast, 1973), pp 86–96.

LETTER FROM AN ORANGEMAN

1. This lengthy article had been carried in the April 1834 edition of the *Dublin University Magazine*. It covered much of the same ground as 'Old Orangeman', arguing that the Orange Order was a defence against Catholic secret society aggression and consistently loyal to the Crown.
2. The Defenders were established in County Armagh in 1784 as a response to the depredation of the Protestant Peep o'Day Boys, who were raiding Catholic homes in the district. It was largely but not entirely Catholic. In the 1790s, it would provide the framework for much of the United Irishman revolutionary 'army'.
3. Dr James Stuart (1764–1840) was author of a *History of Armagh* (1821). His bi-weekly newspaper, *The Guardian and Constitutional Advocate*, published between 1827 and 1836, took a conservative and Protestant stance 'for the avowed purpose of counteracting the teaching of the (Northern) Whig', Belfast's leading liberal paper. John S. North, *The Waterloo Directory of Irish Newspapers and Periodicals, 1800–1900* (Waterloo, 1986), p. 231.
4. The Orange Order was established immediately following the 'Battle of the Diamond', a collision between Defenders and Peep o'Day Boys near Portadown in County Armagh, on 21 September 1795.
5. Sir Richard Musgrave (c. 1757–1818) was a member for Lismore of the old Irish Parliament from 1778 to 1801. In 1782, he was created a baronet. He authored a lurid but amply evidenced *Memoirs of the Different Rebellions in Ireland*, which was a key part of the anti-Catholic interpretation of the 1798 Rebellion. Francis Hardy edited *Memoirs of the Earl of Charlemont* (1810). As commander-in-chief of the Volunteers, Charlemont was in close touch with affairs in Armagh. Sectarian disorder was sparked by a struggle over who

should own Volunteer arms, the Peep o'Day Boys raiding Catholic homes believed to be in possession. James Verner (1746–1822), MP for Dungannon and high Sherriff of County Armagh, had led a detachment of the North Mayo militia to cut off a Defender party seeking to join the fray at the Battle of the Diamond. Though he never joined, he was friendly to the Orange Order.

6. Dyan (Dian) is a townland in County Tyrone. James Alexander (1730–1802) had made a fortune as a 'nabob' merchant and administrator in India. He bought the Caledon estate in County Tyrone and County Armagh in 1776 and sat in the United Kingdom House of Lords from 1801 as 1st Earl of Caledon. He was a strong Tory, sympathetic to Orange principles.

7. The Dyan Lodge received the No. 1 warrant by lot, while the first Lodge to organise had actually been in Loughgall.

8. The Volunteers were an armed citizen body, usually under gentry control, formed in Belfast in 1778. They quickly became political, supporting the independence of the Irish parliament from parliament in London. They were suppressed in 1793.

9. James (rather than Thomas) Wilson was a substantial Presbyterian farmer connected to the Peep o'Day Boys. Eager to win the sympathy of the local Church of Ireland clergy, the newly established Orange Order preferred to give its nominal leadership to the respectable James Sloane, proprietor of an inn in Loughgall.

10. This appears to be an editorial invention. It had no status as a 'fundamental rule'.

11. This would give Old Orangeman a birth date of 1748.

12. Old Orangeman later names the leading 'demagogues and incendiaries' as Joseph Hume, John Arthur Roebuck, Daniel O'Connell, and Whittle Harvey. Joseph Hume (1777–1855), Radical MP for Middlesex, had cooperated with Daniel O'Connell in establishing the pro-democracy Metropolitan Political Union in March 1830. He had been a vocal critic of the Orange Order since 1823, and was a moving spirit in the appointment of a Select Committee to expose, as he hoped, its destructive activities. John Arthur Roebuck (1801–1879) was a lawyer and MP, first elected for Bath in 1832. Though outspokenly Radical, he was a strong supporter of the Union between Britain and Ireland. Daniel O'Connell (1775–1847), the 'Liberator', led the struggle for Catholic Emancipation in the 1820s, Catholic civil rights and Radicalism in general in the 1830s, and Repeal of the Act of Union in the 1840s. He was in general a strong opponent of the Orange Order, though willing if possible to effect an understanding with it. Daniel Whittle Harvey (1786–1863) was a moderate Radical MP, first elected for Colchester in 1818. He founded the *Sunday Times*.

13. On 23 March 1835, the House of Commons ordered that a Select Committee be appointed to inquire into the nature, character, extent and tendency of Orange Lodges, Associations, or Societies in Ireland, with the power to send for persons, papers and records. It was to report back to the House.

14. Old Orangeman here refers to the international impact of the French Revolution. By the *Décret du 19 Novembre 1792*, the French National Convention, having abolished the monarchy at home and already at war with the powers of old regime Europe, declared that 'the French nation offers its fraternal assistance to all peoples who wish to recover their liberty.'

15. *Fons et origo* is a Latin phrase meaning 'source and origin', often used to describe the starting point or the original cause of something. The author is denying that that the origins of sectarian animosity can be traced to the Orange Order.

16. The 'party' Old Orangeman has in mind comprised the supporters of Catholic civil liberties in Ireland and Radicals in Great Britain.

17. According to the Book of Genesis, of course, Cain killed Abel: in fallen humanity's first murder.

18. 1794 saw the culmination of the French Revolution's most radical phase, with the Terror regime of the Jacobins overcoming the threat of foreign conquest and driving both Spain and Prussia out of the alliance arrayed against France (Austria and England remained in arms). The Jacobins were overthrown in July and the 'Directory' took power. In Ireland, the militancy of the largely Catholic and peasant-based Defender secret society was rapidly spreading its influence, raiding for arms and manufacturing its own supply of pikes. The United Irishmen organisation, as it became more seriously revolutionary, developed close links with Defenderism.

19. The reference is William Blake's poem, 'The Song of Los', published in 1795. Mount Hekla is a volcano in Iceland and Mount Chimborazo a volcano in Ecuador. Blake, who was deeply inspired by the American and French Revolutions, was evoking a sense of global, volcanic revolution.

20. Henry Grattan (1746–1820) was leader of the 'Patriot' party in the Irish House of Commons which, in 1782, had wrested from England 'Irish independence', meaning the sole right of the Irish Parliament to legislate for the nation. The executive Government of Ireland, usually referred to as 'Dublin Castle', remained responsible to the King's ministers in London and by corrupt practices could usually push its preferred legislation through the Irish Parliament.

21. Poynings' Law (1494–95), also known as the Statute of Drogheda, forbade the Irish Parliament from passing or discussing legislation without the approval of the English Crown and Privy Council. Henry Grattan and

the Irish Patriot Party succeeded in having Poynings' Law repealed in 1782, achieving 'legislative independence'. By the 'Commercial Propositions' of 1785, Prime Minister William Pitt had proposed free trade between Britain and Ireland. These had been opposed by the Irish Patriot Party as an infringement of Ireland's right to regulate its own external trade relations. The controversy raised the spectre of an Irish Parliament pursuing its own foreign policy independent of Britain, an ambition made explicit by Patriot radicals. Pitt's scheme collapsed in part because of the hostility of English business interests.

22. Prospero, the magician-king figure of Shakespeare's play, *The Tempest*, had the ability to control the elements and raise storms at will.

23. Edmund Burke (1729–1797), an Irish born parliamentarian, intellectual and controversialist, was sympathetic to Catholic claims but violently hostile to democratic tendencies. Henry Flood (1732–1791), sometime rival to Grattan as leader of the Patriot Party, was hostile to Catholic claims but favourable towards greater Protestant democracy. John Philpott Curran (1750–1817) was a Patriot parliamentarian of radical tendency who, as a lawyer, defended at trial many United Irishmen.

24. Enthusiasm for both the American and the French Revolutions was most powerfully felt in Presbyterian Ulster. It appealed both to its secularising liberal 'New Light' tendency and its millenarian 'Old Light' tendency, which applauded the apparent downfall of Roman Catholicism in its French stronghold.

25. 'Out of Doors' referred to public petitioning, demonstrations and riots in support of or in opposition to measures before the Irish parliament. In the Volunteers it took an organised and armed form, and substantially added weight to the Patriot Party.

26. In May 1797, despairing of Government reaction and the drift towards repression, Grattan withdrew from parliament.

27. Ossian, a pastiche of Gaelic mythology published as if genuine by the Scottish writer James Macpherson in the 1760s, enjoyed a European-wide popularity and did much to promote a particularly romantic and mysterious conception of the 'Celtic nature'.

28. From 1792, Grattan had favoured the extension of the franchise to Catholics (conceded in 1793) and their admission into Parliament. He was expected to be a close advisor to Viceroy Lord Fitzwilliam in forwarding this project before the latter's sudden dismissal by the London Government in 1795, an episode that demoralised Grattan and radicalised Irish 'out of doors' opposition.

29. The Penal Laws were a succession of Acts passed between 1695 and 1709 by Westminster and the exclusively protestant Irish Parliament to

permanently subordinate Catholics, who were excluded from crown offices, forbidden to purchase land or take a lease for longer than 31 years or practice law. Catholic education was outlawed and Catholics were forbidden to own a horse worth more than five pounds. Catholics lost the right to vote and be elected to parliament. As the dissenters of Ireland – most notably the Presbyterians of Ulster – were also outside the state religion, they too were discriminated against, but to a lesser extent.

30. Before the opening of a state-aided Catholic seminary at Maynooth, County Kildare, in 1795, Catholic clergy were educated on the continent.

31. The established church in Ireland were relatively slow to adopt the evangelical revival but by the early years of the nineteenth century it had become by far the most evangelical section of the Anglican Communion.

32. Spoken by Mary Magdalene upon finding the tomb of Jesus empty. John 20:13.

33. Book of Proverbs, chapter 4, verse 18.

34. 'Latitudinarian' was a term for those who favoured a doctrinally 'broad' Established Church, but in this context implies anyone lacking sufficient hostility to Roman Catholicism.

35. Daniel O'Connell and Richard Lalor Sheil (1791–1851). Sheil was a founder member and talented propagandist for the Catholic Association. He was unenthusiastic in following O'Connell in seeking Repeal of the Union and served as a junior minister in Whig Governments. He was MP for Tipperary from 1833.

36. The 'Catholic Rent' referred both to subscription fees to the Catholic Association and successor organisations, and specific collections to help O'Connell's defray his political expenses. O'Connell was often accused, unfairly, of cynical demagoguery to raise 'rent' for his personal aggrandisement.

37. The Pennefathers, Jacksons, Scotts, Littons and Brookes were prominent names in Irish legal, Evangelical and Orange circles. Edward Litton (1787–1870) was an Irish barrister and Conservative MP, later Master in Chancery. Baron Richard Pennefather (1773–1859) was an Irish judge and chief baron of the exchequer in Ireland; he was considered to be relatively impartial but not a talented jurist.

38. The phrase 'good conscience', drawn from classical and biblical sources, was a common term in the legal-religious discourse of English and Anglo-Irish Protestantism. The implication was that the word of Roman Catholics could not be trusted, as they could seek absolution for crime, deceit and oath-breaking in the confessional.

39. 'Papism' was the preferred term for Roman Catholicism in Protestant circles, as Anglicanism claimed to be the true universal ('Catholic') church

and Roman Catholicism was not considered to be a church properly speaking, instead being an extension of the pope's temporal power.

40. A paraphrase of Galatians 5:1.

41. Reference to 1 Corinthians 12:31, where St. Paul offers 'a more excellent way' than simply miraculous powers (prophecy, healing, speaking tongues etc.): love and charity in Christ.

42. 'Seven other spirits' is a reference to Matthew 12:43–45, where Jesus warns that mental soul-cleansing without commitment to a positive faith will only end in relapse and even worse corruption.

43. Old Orangeman has in mind here the numerous peasant leagues – Rockites, Ribbonmen, Blackfeet and so on – generally known by the appellation *buachaillí* or 'boys'.

44. The Catholic Mass, of course, was in Latin, and the faithful were discouraged from reading the bible directly, for fear of misinterpreting it.

45. Second Epistle to Timothy, ch. 3, verse 15, where Paul recommends knowledge of the Holy Scriptures.

46. 'The leaven that was hid in three measures of meal' is a reference to a parable by Jesus in Matthew 13:33, where he assures his disciples that the 'kingdom of heaven' they embody on earth, from its small beginnings, can transform the world.

47. 'Will worship' (Greek: *ethelothreskeia*) refers to self-imposed or invented religious practices – forms of worship that are based on human will or ideas rather than divine command. Colossians 2:23.

48. John 4:24, where Jesus asserts that true worship is not tied to physical locations (like a temple or mountain) but must come from the heart (spirit) and be sincere and aligned with God's truth.

49. It was central to Reformation theology that salvation was not to be acquired through 'good works' but by 'faith alone' (*sola fide*).

50. 'Root out and destroy' is a reference to Jeremiah 1:10, which was often taken as a biblical authority for persecuting and extirpating heresy through force and terror.

51. 'Extermination' in the first-half of the nineteenth century did not have the inevitable sense of killing, but usually referred to forcible removal or expulsion. It was often used in reference to evictions, for example.

52. Charity 'thinketh no evil'. 1 Corinthians 13:5.

53. This alludes to the 'exclusive salvation' doctrine of Catholicism – *Extra Ecclesiam nulla salus* ('Outside the Church there is no salvation') – which implicitly condemned to perdition all those outside the Roman Church. It had fallen into some desuetude, but was reasserted by the post-Napoleonic Papacy. Its exclusivity was dropped by the Church at the time of Vatican II in 1964 (*Lumen Gentium*).

54. A perhaps unexpected quotation from the patriot and radical lawyer, John Philpott Curran, in his defence of Owen Kirwan, a participant in Robert Emmet's rebellion of 1803, at his trial for high treason. Curran had been claiming that the 'bigotry' arising from genuine belief in 'exclusive salvation' was a thing of the past. In May 1824, however, Pope Leo XII issued an encyclical letter, *Ubi Primum*, re-stating that 'out of the Church there is no salvation' and he was echoed even more forcefully by a statement published by the Catholic hierarchy of Ireland.
55. A reference to *vis medicatrix naturae*, a dictum of Hippocratic medicine, that a body can usually heal itself.
56. Old Orangeman refers here to the protestant, largely Presbyterian secret society, the Peep-o'Day Boys, established in July 1784, which raided and expelled Catholic homes in County Armagh. Many had been former Volunteers.
57. A reference to the Defenders, a largely Catholic peasant league which resisted and retaliated against Peep-o'Day depredations.
58. The famous 'Battle of the Diamond' took place on 21 December 1794.
59. Joseph Atkinson of Crowhill, a local landlord, had commanded the protestant side at the Diamond fight.
60. This well-known phrase was attributed to the Cromwellians of the 1650s when they transplanted those Catholic landowners not altogether dispossessed, along with many of their tenants and followers, to inferior holdings in the west of Ireland. The initial Cromwellian plan, deemed impracticable, had been to sweep the entirety of the Catholic population into Connacht.
61. The phrase 'wade knee deep in Protestant blood' was ascribed to a Whitefeet oath by Col. Verner, the Orange leader, in 1835. Its authenticity may be doubted.
62. William III, Prince of Orange (a title he held as the stadtholder, or national leader of the Dutch Republic) had been ascended to the throne of England in the Glorious Revolution of 1689. He was a hero in protestant Ireland and the term 'Orange' was long associated with supporters of Protestant Ascendancy in Ireland.
63. It was estimated that about 700 Catholic families, or 4,000 persons, were driven from County Armagh to Connacht by 'Orange' intimidation and attack. A smaller number of Presbyterians, sympathetic to the United Irishmen, were chased off to Belfast.
64. In August 1798, about 1,000 French soldiers landed in County Mayo, where they were joined by many Catholic peasants. After initial military success they were forced to surrender. French soldiers were taken as prisoners of war while their Irish peasant auxiliaries were massacred.

65. Theobald Wolfe Tone (1763–1798), founder member of the United Irishmen and its primary liaison with the revolutionary French Government.
66. Thomas Paine (1737–1809), a revolutionary thinker, republican, democrat and free-thinker.
67. Only bad weather prevented French General Lazare Hoche from landing 43 ships and 15,000 troops at Bantry Bay, County Cork, in December 1796.
68. He means, why Catholics are excluded from the Orange Order.
69. Archibald Hamilton Rowan (1751–1834) was an Ulster Presbyterian, a founder member of the United Irishmen, and a life-long radical. His son, in contrast, would be an early leader of the conservative turn in Ulster Presbyterianism. James Napper Tandy (1740–1803) was a leader of Dublin radicalism and an important link-man between the United Irishmen and the Defenders. John Keogh (1740–1817) was a Dublin merchant and the main link-man between the Catholic Committee and the United Irishmen. Along with Grattan and Tone, all the men Old Orangeman mentions here, with the exception of Keogh, were protestant.
70. Robert Emmet (1778–1803), a second-echelon figure in the United Irishmen in the late 1790s, attempted to lead a separatist rebellion in Dublin in 1803. He was found guilty of high treason and executed. His moving speech from the dock and youthful romanticism assured him a legendary afterlife. The Lord Chancellor of Ireland in 1834 was William Conyngham Plunket, 1st Baron Plunket (1764–1854), best known for having prosecuted Emmet.
71. In October 1816, freelance raiders for murky reasons attacked and set on fire Wildgoose Lodge in County Louth. Eight people, a family and their relatives, died in the flames. Eighteen suspects, at least nine certainly innocent, were executed after trial. Protestant opinion blamed peasant-nationalist Ribbonism for the attack.
72. Thomas Russell (1767–1803), a protestant ally of Wolfe Tone, had attempted without success to raise Ulster in support of Emmet's rebellion, and was executed for High treason.
73. Born a Catholic, Mortimer O'Sullivan (1791–1859) converted to the Church of Ireland in his youth. A member of the Orange Order, he had a prominent career as an anti-Catholic controversialist. He was a leading figure behind the Orange and Conservative but culturally patriotic and intellectually significant *Dublin University Magazine*.
74. François Thurot, a French naval officer and licensed privateer, raided the port of Carrickfergus, County Antrim, in 1760, during the Seven Years' War (1756–1763). The revealed possibility of invasion, and the weakness of British military forces in Ireland, quickly spread the recently established Volunteers, with lukewarm approval from the Government.

75. Rev. William Jackson (c. 1737–1795), an Anglo-Irish Anglican clergyman and radical, acted as an agent for the French Government when he met with United Irish leaders in 1794. Along with Wolfe Tone, he was exposed by an English spy, John Cockayne. Wolfe Tone was allowed to leave Ireland while Jackson, put on trial for high treason, died in the dock, having apparently taken poison shortly beforehand.
76. Supporters of the Orange Order habitually 'walked' in procession every July, particularly on the 'Twelfth' to commemorate the defeat of the Catholic Jacobite armies in Ireland at the Battle of the Boyne in 1690, and to assert continuing Protestant Ascendancy.
77. By 'unemancipated', Old Orangeman seems to be recalling the years before qualified Catholics were granted the suffrage in 1793 rather than their admission to the Parliament of the United Kingdom in 1829.
78. The Holy Day commemorating Ireland's national saint, Patrick, was usually marked by Catholic and nationalist marching.
79. The Party Processions Act of 1832 (2 & 3 William IV c. 118) banned political and 'sectarian' marches in Ireland; also the display of 'party' colours and emblems. It was much resented by the Orange Order as suggesting their equivalence to 'disloyal' manifestations.
80. Lord Stanley (1799–1869) at this time was Chief Secretary for Ireland.
81. Sir Robert Peel (1788–1850) had been Chief Secretary for Ireland between 1812 and 1818, when he had indulged Orange coat-trailing, and at this time was leader of the Conservative Opposition to the Whig Government at Westminster.
82. It was a common Reformation assertion that the Roman Catholic Church permitted the faithful to deceive and break oaths compacted with heretics (i.e. protestants). This had no basis in Catholic canon law, as 'Old Orangemen' seems to implicitly allow.
83. Old Orangeman discussed the attack on Alexander Barclay at Forkhill near Dundalk in 1789 and the outrage at Wildgoose Lodge in 1816 in his First Letter. The Sheas were the family of Edmund Shea, a large farmer and landlord of Gurtnapisha, County Tipperary, whose premises were set on fire by an unidentified raiding party in November 1821. No less than 16 people died in the blaze, including children, labourers and maidservants. The motive seems to have been agrarian and employment-dispute related rather than sectarian. The massacres of some hundreds of loyalist and mostly protestant prisoners at Scullabogue and Waterford Bridge at the hands of Catholic rebels in that County were notorious episodes of the 1798 Rebellion.
84. Sir Ambrose Hardinge Giffard (1771–1827), a lawyer and for a period acting deputy Grand Master of the Orange Order.

85. William Conyngham Plunket (1764–1854), the prominent lawyer, had shown his impatience with interminable sectarian controversy dragging up past misdeeds when he retorted that 'History is only an old Almanack'.
86. Kings 8:13. The Prophet Elisha tells an incredulous Hazael that he will become king and go on to commit terrible atrocities.
87. Peter Dens (Pierre Dens), *Theologia moralis et dogmatica* (Moral and Dogmatic Theology) was a Roman Catholic theological manual written by a Flemish theologian in the mid-18th century and used to train Irish priests in Maynooth Seminary. Protestant polemicists quoted it selectively to accuse Catholic clergy of imbibing such precepts as 'no faith should be kept with heretics'.
88. Old Orangeman refers here to Catholic resistance to paying tithes on crops as a tax to maintain the clergy of the Church of Ireland. Since 1831, tithe resistance had assumed mass non-payment proportions in a 'Tithe War'. Tithes as an imposition on the peasantry were effectively ended by the Tithe Commutation Act of 1838. As noted above, the term 'extermination' here is better understood as 'removal' or 'expulsion' than killing.
89. It was a Protestant conviction that Catholics used 'good works' as a way of paying off debts to God. Such 'acts of contrition' in paying off sin, it was argued, were a license for wickedness. The Irish peasantry, who had no structure of formal Poor Law before 1838, were well known for their charity to strangers and mutual aid.
90. The Roman Catholic clergy were cautious about the laity bible-reading without the benefit of informed guidance. The preferred form of instruction was the Homily (the priest commenting on bible readings during church service) and the Catechism (a structured exposition of dogma, usually in question-and-answer format). Nevertheless, the Roman Catholic Church did not at this time forbid its members to read the bible without notes.
91. The blood of Januarius, a relic of the saint contained in ampoules, is said to miraculously liquefy three times a year. Protestants assumed trickery.
92. Old Orangeman is referring to the *buachaillí*, or peasant leagues and secret societies, famously described by Sir George Cornewall Lewis in 1836 as akin to 'a vast trades union for the protection of the Irish peasantry'.
93. Probable reference to Satan's words in Milton's *Paradise Lost*, Book IV, line 110.
94. The 'Armagh Orange Canon', copied by all counties, stipulated that Jesus was the 'only Mediator between a sinful creature, and an offended Creator'. Roman Catholics who looked also to other mediators, such as saints and clergy, 'can be no Christian', and as such were necessarily excluded from the Orange Order. See Member of the Order [R. M. Sibbett], *Orangeism in Ireland and throughout the Empire*, vol. I (London, n.d. [1939]), p 337.

95. Old Orangeman seems to be torturing Sheil's purely empirical observation that the powerful Orange Order was a 'confederacy … exclusively sectarian' and 'an enormous mass of organized Protestantism … in arms'. Sheil called for the Orange Order to be suppressed, not made accessible to Catholics. See 'Orange Lodges: Speech in the House of Commons, August 11, 1835' in Thomas MacNevin (ed), *The Speeches of the Right Honourable Richard Lalor Sheil* (Dublin, 1872), p. 121, p. 125. However, Old Orangeman was correct that the sectarian exclusivity of the Orange Order presented an exposed flank. When the Select Committee on the Orange Order reported, William IV, for the Government, declared his determination 'to take measures for the effectual discouragement of Orange Lodges, and of *all political societies excluding persons of a different religious faith*, using secret signs and symbols, and acting by means of associated branches.' [My emphasis] The Order dissolved itself before action could be taken.
96. For O'Connell's view that Ribbonism was 'a continuation of the Defender system', by which he seems to have meant in form and substance rather than organisational continuity, see *First Report from the Select Committee on the State Of Ireland: 1825, Ordered, by The House of Commons, to be Printed, 23 March 1825*, p. 71.
97. He is referring to the province of Ulster in the north of Ireland.
98. This refers to the disorders arising from the Tithe War. Much of that conflict was concentrated in south Leinster and Munster.
99. This was a principal concern for the Select Committee on Orange Lodges.
100. He seems to have in mind Sheil's speech referenced above.
101. This was a reference to British army regiments holding orange warrants (that is, maintaining an Orange Lodge). There were thirty-two such regiments in 1830, about a fifth of all regiments.
102. No United Irishmen 'Assassination Committee' as such existed, though dangerous magistrates and informers were targeted by Defender groups in particular, and the Dublin *Union Star* newspaper, edited by Walter Cox in 1797, openly promoted assassination as a tactic.
103. *Report from the Select Committee appointed to inquire into the nature, character, extent and tendency of Orange Lodges, Associations or Societies in Ireland; with the minutes of evidence, and appendix, Ordered, by The House of Commons to be Printed, 20 July 1835*, pp 195–6.
104. Archibald Acheson, 2nd Earl of Gosford (1771–1827), Lord Lieutenant of County Armagh. His 'tertium quid' (mediation) was as follows: 'I am not against the Orangemen of the country, for I think they are a very fine race of men as can be … [But] when they band themselves into political associations, it is those associations that I am opposed to, as being injurious to the peace and tranquillity of the country … I am against the principles

on which they act. … I think that all associations, whether Ribbonmen or Orangemen, are bad in themselves and dangerous to the State.' *Report from the Select Committee appointed to inquire into the nature, character, extent and tendency of Orange Lodges, Associations or Societies in Ireland; with the minutes of evidence, and appendix, Ordered, by The House of Commons to be Printed, 20 July 1835*, p. 276.

105. Gosford did not, in fact, approve Orange principles as a whole.

106. Sir Jonah Barrington (1760–1834), Irish judge and memoirist. See his *Historic Memoirs of Ireland: Comprising Secret Records of the National Convention, the Rebellion, and the Union*, vol. I (London: Henry Colburn, 1835), p. 53.

107. 'Q. Do you not believe, that the Roman Catholic population in Dublin used to turn out, and go round the statue of King William on his birth day? — A. Yes; the Catholics at that period, fired over the statue of King William, and joined in it heartily.' O'Connell's evidence as printed in *First Report from the Select Committee on the State Of Ireland: 1825, Ordered, by The House of Commons, to be Printed, 23 March 1825*, p. 69.

108. Thomas Knox, Lord Northland (1754–1840), a County Down landlord. Until the mid-1770s he was considered to be close to the Patriot opposition to Dublin Castle. He joined the Dublin Lodge of the Orange Order in June 1796. William Brownlow (1755–1815), a County Armagh landlord and banker, repudiated the Patriot views of his father and became an early patron of the Orange Order in his county.

109. Francis Plowden (1749–1829) was an English-born Catholic lawyer, historian, and political writer. He strongly supported Catholic emancipation and Irish rights. Threat of legal action for libel from Dublin Castle forced him into exile to France. See his polemic, *Historical Disquisition concerning the Orange Societies in Ireland* (Dublin: R. Coyne, 1810).

110. Rev. Mortimer O'Sullivan, *Case of the Protestants Of Ireland, Stated in Addresses Delivered at Meetings in Dublin, Liverpool, Bristol, and Bath, in the Year 1834* (London; John Hatchard, 1836), pp 39–42.

111. John Lawless (c.1773–1837), was a Catholic nationalist and journalist from Belfast. His attempt to lead a march north in the tense period between O'Connell's victory in the Clare by-election in July 1828 and the Government's eventual capitulation on the question of Catholic emancipation was felt by many to have brought the island close to civil war.

112. Thomas Wyse (1791–1862) was a wealthy Waterford Catholic who was a close ally to O'Connell in the Catholic Association and an important strategist of the Emancipation struggle. He declined to follow O'Connell in calling for Repeal of the Union. See his *Historical Sketch of the Late Catholic Association of Ireland* (London: Henry Colburn, 1829).

113. 'Reconciliation meetings' were organised by the Catholic association to bring together contending *buachaillí* factions. They probably did as much to organise and discipline as to pacify and subordinate them.
114. This refers to the unwritten laws of the countryside maintained by the *buachaillí* societies.
115. At a public banquet in Clonmel in September 1828, O'Connell had responded to rumours of Orangemen planning a 'new '98' with the cry, 'Would to God that our excellent Viceroy Lord Anglesey would but give me a commission, and if those men of blood should attempt to attack the property and persons of His Majesty's loyal subjects, with a hundred thousand of my brave Tipperary boys I would soon drive them into the sea!'
116. The episode at Ballibay took place on 23 September 1828.
117. Samuel Gray (1782–1848) was a notorious Orange gang leader and virtual dictator in the Ballybay area. In 1841, he was acquitted of murder by a jury packed with Orangemen. His son, James, was transported for jury-tampering.
118. In fact a number of attacks were made on Catholics and one, Patrick Harkin, was killed.
119. The title given by the Catholic association to such representatives, tasked with trying to suppress sectarian and *buachaillí* outbreaks, was 'Pacificator'.
120. Muster was a stronghold of *buachaillí* secret societies.
121. Famously, 300 Spartans had held off tens of thousands of Persian 'barbarians' at the Pass of Thermopylae in 480BC.
122. Constantine Henry Phipps, Lord Mulgrave (1797–1863) was appointed Lord Lieutenant of Ireland in April 1835. His predecessor, Richard Wellesley, suspected of a desire to clip the wings of the Orange Order, was jeered and had drinks thrown at him when he visited the Royal Theatre in Dublin on 14 December 1822; the notorious 'bottle and rattle riot'.
123. As police cut down Orange bunting in loyalist Sandy Row they came into collision with the crowd. Annie Moore and William Trainer were killed by police fire.
124. The first significant sectarian riot had taken place in Belfast on 22 December 1832, when a loyalist mob attacked the mainly Catholic Hercules Street. Four people were killed by policemen.
125. Old Orangeman is thinking of the Whig Government which had introduced and passed, in the teeth of ferocious Tory opposition, the Great Reform Act of 1832, somewhat extending the franchise. England came as close to revolution as it ever would in the modern era.
126. This rather obscure passage paraphrases an episode in the life of John Knox (c. 1514–1572), the militant Calvinist reformer and founder of Presbyterianism. During reign of Mary, Queen of Scots, Knox had attempted

to mobilise nobles to defend protestant rioters arrested by the Crown. He was summoned to Edinburgh Castle in May 1563 to answer charges of treason. Here, in the presence of Mary, the Catholic monarch of a protestant kingdom, he reminded his accusers that he was simply repeating what they had said in different circumstances. The treason case was allowed to drop. See Thomas M'Crie, *The Life of John Knox*, 2nd ed. ii (Edinburgh, 1813), pp 95–106.

127. The adage of the bundle of sticks was a reference to the Roman *fasces*, a bundle of sticks tightly bound together: a symbol of strength in unity.

128. Old Orangeman had two causes for concern. First, Presbyterians were no happier about paying tithes to the Church of Ireland than Catholics and there was a potential for interdenominational rupture of protestant Ireland on the question. Second, British ministers regularly considered ways by which the Roman Catholic Church in Ireland might be surreptitiously endowed by the state so as to secure its loyalty. If this seemed likely, militant protestants might be inclined to support a restoration of the Irish Parliament, thus repealing the Act of Union, as a firebreak from British meddling.

129. By 'garrison', Old Orangeman means the protestant and landlord ascendancy in Ireland, the bulwark of English power in the country.

130. This refers to the Church of Ireland. Its maintenance in perpetuity as the Established religion in Ireland had been included in the 1800 Act of Union which created the United Kingdom of Great Britain and Ireland.

131. This refers to the popular campaign of tithe non-payment, resistance, and intimidation directed against the clergy and agents of the Church of Ireland.

132. Psalm 57:1.

133. Old Orangeman here refers not just to organisation such as the Catholic Association, but the radical 'Political Unions', both middle class and working class, that had sprung up in Britain to press for suffrage reform.

134. The Volunteer movement was formed in 1778 to protect Ireland from foreign invasion but within a year were adding their strength to the Patriot opposition to British policies for Ireland.

135. A reference to the Great Reform Act of 1832, which systematised parliamentary representation and expanded the enfranchised population in England by about 50 per cent, so that one in five adult men in England could vote.

136. An 'infernal machine' was a term usually applied to bombs or gun-traps used to assassinate leading political figures.

137. A reference to the Robert Emmet rebellion.

138. The Carthaginian general Hannibal destroyed the army of the Roman Republic at Cannae in 216BC. Hannibal's forces wintered at Capua rather

than marching on to Rome itself and while luxuriating here, according to Livy, they lost their edge.

139. The Orange Order had formally dissolved itself following passage of the Unlawful Oaths Act in July 1825. In August 1828 the Brunswick Protestant Clubs were launched to counter O'Connell's Catholic Association (which had been remodelled to evade the 1825 Act). 'The agencies created by the Orangemen, called Brunswick clubs, were modelled on the Liberal clubs established by O'Connell prior to the Clare election. They were recruited from among former Orangemen, and listed among their patrons a substantial number of Orange peers, headed by the earl of Enniskillen. The local Brunswick clubs were drawn mostly from the lower classes, but dominated by parliamentarians, lawyers, and clergy of the established church.' Hereward Senior, *Orangeism in Ireland and Britain, 1795–1836* (London: Routledge & Kegan Paul, 1966), p. 225.

140. Quote a paraphrase of Shakespeare's *Romeo and Juliet*, Act 3, Scene 1.

141. Exodus 7:10–12. Aaron's rod becomes a serpent before Pharaoh, swallowing the rods of the Egyptian magicians.

142. Book of Numbers, 16: 48. Aaron, as high priest, ran into a raging plague to atone for the sins of the people. In so doing, he stopped the spread of infection.

143. As laid down in the Order's rules and regulations, meetings opened and closed with prayer. The opening prayer include the lines, 'Gracious and Almighty God, who in all ages has shown thy mighty power in protecting righteous kings and states, we yield thee hearty thanks for so miraculously bringing to light and frustrating the secret and horrible designs of our enemies, plotted and intended to have been executed against our gracious King, our happy constitution, and the true religion established by our glorious deliverer, William the Third, Prince of Orange. Vouchsafe, O Lord, to continue unto us thine almighty protection; grant to our pious King, long life, health and prosperity; let thy providence ever guard our happy constitution, and enable us to transmit it to our latest posterity, unimpaired, and improved by our holy religion.' (Or a variation thereof). The closing prayer included the lines, 'O Almighty God, who art a strong tower of defence unto thy servants, against the face of their enemies; we yield thee praise and thanks for our deliverance from those great and apparent dangers wherewith we were encompassed: we acknowledge thy goodness that we were not delivered over as a prey unto them, beseeching thee still to continue such thy mercies towards us, that all the world may know thou art our Saviour and mighty Deliverer, through Jesus Christ. Amen.' The objection was that it cast a religious veil over an essentially secular institution and sanctified belligerence. It was held to licence Orange violence and prejudice.

144. In ancient Rome, the priestesses of the temple were tasked with keeping the vestal fire permanently alight, for the safety of the state.
145. The Radical MP Joseph Hume quoted Rev. Mortimer O'Sullivan at length on the elaborate ritual of Orange induction and commented: 'Was not this a profanation of the Scriptures? What were the details of these Orange Lodges? They might truly be said to be written in blood. They arrogated to themselves the assumption that they exclusively were Protestants, and they censured and condemned all who did not follow the course they marked out. A great portion of the police in Ireland were Orangemen, and it was impossible that they could discharge their duty with impartiality, or that they would forget the ties that bound them in this brotherhood. It was not possible that the people should rest satisfied as long as this state of things continued.' *House of Commons Debates*, 4 Aug. 1835, cols 64–5.
146. In an uncharacteristic eruption of hysteria, Old Orangeman seems to be implying here that Hume was a servant of Satan.
147. Gospel of John, 3: 20–21.
148. In an open letter from Lord Stanley (1799–1869), formerly Whig Chief Secretary of Ireland, to Sir Thomas Hesketh, Chairman of the North Lancashire Conservative Association, published in the *Morning Chronicle* of 18 June 1835, Stanley had warned that local Conservative associations being organised in Britain on the Orange model must inevitably provoke counter-organisation by radicals. He predicted that such organisations would seek to 'oppress by combination' the elected members of the House of Commons.
149. Lord Grey (1764–1845), Whig leader and Prime Minister when the Great Reform Act was introduced and enacted.
150. The Whig Government, under pressure from O'Connell, argued for 'appropriation' of a certain amount of surplus funds attaching to the Church of Ireland for socially useful purposes. By the Lichfield House Compact of February 1835, O'Connell's party and the Whigs agreed to cooperate to this end. Lord Stanley, a strong advocate of Anglicanism, had broken with the Whigs in 1834 over the issue and by the late 1830s had merged his group into the Conservative Party, which he would go on to lead. The Conservatives made great play of the 'appropriation' issue in the country and by 1838 the Whigs had given up trying to drive it through.
151. 'If Troy could have been saved, [it would have been saved by now.]' Virgil's *Aeneid*, Book 2. Old Orangeman is implying that mere parliamentary defence of the Protestant Ascendancy had reached its limit; it required popular organisation from below, in the form of the Orange Order and kindred popular organisations of resistance.
152. Thomas Attwood's 'Birmingham Political Union', the most prominent such radical Union; the National Union of the Working Classes (founded

in 1831, and abandoned in 1835); the London-based National Reform Association, a precursor to the Chartists. They had all played a role in driving through passage of the Great Reform Act.

153. Paraphrase of Job 38:11.

154. Odysseus and his men were trapped in the cave of Polyphemus, the cannibal giant Cyclopes. Odysseus cunningly engineered their escape by making Polyphemus drunk and blinding him in his one eye with a stake. Homer's *Odyssey*, Book 9.

155. Samuel Taylor Coleridge (1772–1834), a romantic poet and, latterly, a conservative intellectual. 'The English people are at present like a person who is so sensitively alive to pain in some morbid part of the body, that he cannot feel any injury done to any other member. Nothing can be more disgraceful than their foreign conduct for the last four years; but nothing that can be said on the subject seems to produce the least impression on them.' Coleridge quoted in 'Foreign Policy', *Blackwood's Edinburgh Magazine*, August 1835, p. 205.

156. This refers to the Lichfield House Compact, an informal alliance between Whig ministers and O'Connell's party.

157. To 'strike colours' was for a ship to lower its flag as a signal of surrender.

158. Psalm 46:5.

159. Psalm 57:1.

160. A reference to the 'Siege of Derry' (1689), when heroic resistance prevented Catholic Jacobite forces capturing the city.

161. The Conservatives had made large gains in the General Election of January 1835. They would continue to win ground in the General Election of 1837 and secure a majority in 1841.

162. 'Yeomen' referred to substantial and comfortable farmers. 'Old Orangemen' is seeking to differentiate protestant agriculturalists from the Catholic peasantry, though sociologically the distinction was far from clear.

163. Exeter Hall was a large public meeting place on the north side of the Strand in central London. In June 1835, ultra-Tories connected to the burgeoning Conservative Associations had convened to prove 'to Protestants of all denominations, from authentic documents, the real tenets of the Church of Rome, as now held by the Roman Catholic bishops and priests of Ireland.' *Authentic Report of the Great Protestant meeting held at Exeter Hall, London, on Saturday, June 20, 1835* (Dublin: P. Dixon Hardy, 1835), p. 3.

164. The reformed franchise required that voters be registered as qualified. Much political organisation involved maximising the registration of one's own supporters and questioning the validity for the register of one's opponents. 'Hustings' were public meetings to address electors.

165. A single quote, interpolated, Proverbs 14:34.

166. William Shakespeare, specifically from *Othello*, Act 2, Scene 1.
167. Paraphrase of 1 Peter 2:15.
168. During the crisis leading up to the Great Reform Act, the Duke of Cumberland, the king's son and Imperial Grand Master of the Orange Order, had attempted to rally ultra-Tory resistance around the Order. It is certainly the case that Lieutenant-Colonel William Blennerhasset Fairman, set to the task of organising this initiative, raised the possibility of Cumberland being made Regent and summoning a counter-revolutionary government of resistance.
169. Cork Conservatives, 'a Committee of Orangemen', narrowly took control of Cork Corporation in January 1835, but were unseated on petition. See Ian d'Alton, *Protestant Society and Politics in Cork, 1812–1844* (Cork, 1980), pp 169–70.